THE CRITIC AND THE DRAMA

Another Book of the Theatre

Art of the Night

The Autobiography of an Attitude

Bottoms Up, An Application of the Slapstick to Satire

Comedians All

The Critic and the Drama

Encyclopedia of the Theatre

The Entertainment of a Nation

Europe After 8:15

Materia Critica

The Morning After the First Night

Mr. George Jean Nathan Presents

Passing Judgments

The Popular Theatre

Since Ibsen

Testament of a Critic

The Theatre Book of the Year 1942–43

The Theatre Book of the Year 1943–44

The Theatre Book of the Year 1944–45

The Theatre Book of the Year 1945–46

The Theatre Book of the Year 1946–47

The Theatre Book of the Year 1947–48

The Theatre Book of the Year 1948–49

The Theatre Book of the Year 1949–50

The Theatre in the Fifties

The Theatre of the Moment

The Theatre, The Drama, The Girls

The World in Falseface

THE · CRITIC · AND
THE · DRAMA

BY GEORGE JEAN NATHAN

New Introduction by Charles Angoff

RUTHERFORD • MADISON • TEANECK

FAIRLEIGH DICKINSON UNIVERSITY PRESS

Library of Congress Catalogue Card Number: 75-120099

Reprinted 1972

Associated University Presses, Inc.
Cranbury, New Jersey 08512

ISBN 0-8386-7964-1
Printed in the United States of America

WITH HIS PERMISSION

To EDWARD GORDON CRAIG

THE FIRST ÆSTHETICIAN OF THE THEATRE

CONTENTS

CHAPTER

I. AESTHETIC JURISPRUDENCE

II. DRAMA AS AN ART

III. THE PLACE OF THE THEATRE

IV. THE PLACE OF ACTING

V. DRAMATIC CRITICISM

VI. DRAMATIC CRITICISM IN AMERICA

Introduction

By CHARLES ANGOFF

This book, first published in 1922, is one of the few critical books by Nathan that does not deal, at least in part, with the plays of the year. It is almost completely a book of theorizing, even though he says time and again that theorizing is frequently the enemy of sound criticism.

Nathan reveals, first of all, that he is as familiar with the literature of aesthetics, especially that branch concerned with dramatic criticism, as he is with world drama itself. He is at home with Aristotle and William Hazlitt and Croce and Shaw and Carlyle and Gordon Craig and Pascal and Goethe and Anatole France and Nietzsche and Spingarn and Walkley and all others who have written significantly on the theatre. More, he is sufficiently familiar with other arts, especially fiction and music and painting, to call upon them, now and then, to help him emphasize or illuminate a critical point. He also has a fine flair for the apt epigram. "All art," he says, "is a kind of subconscious madness expressed in terms of sanity; criticism is essential to the interpretation of its mysteries, for about everything truly beautiful there is ever something mysterious and disconcerting." Of course, art is independent of criticism, but criticism "illuminates the enveloping darkness in which art might otherwise rest only vaguely discernible, and perhaps altogether unseen."

The Goethe-Carlyle doctrine that the critic need only determine what the artist had in mind and judge whether he has succeeded in his purpose, seems a bit naïve to

Nathan. He did not believe finally in this or that "theory" of criticism. What he did believe was that "there may be as many kinds of criticism as there are kinds of art." Rules for the creation of art as of the criticism of it seemed absurd to him: "If art knows no rules, criticism knows no rules." Or, to put it another way, "There are as many sound and apt species of criticism as there are works to be criticized. . . . As every work of art is an entity, a thing in itself, so is every piece of criticism an entity, a thing in itself."

But what is drama? Nathan put little store by the usual definitions. He didn't like to be bound by such "prisons." Which is why his own definition (if it may be called such) is so loose and all-inclusive: "Good drama is anything that interests an intelligently emotional group of persons assembled together in an illuminated hall." He points out that "Great drama, like great men and great women, is always just a little sad. Only idiots may be completely happy." If great drama has any "mission" at all—and Nathan was not at all sure of that—it is "not to make numbskulls glad that they are alive, but to make them speculate why they are permitted to be alive at all. . . . The aim of great drama is not to make men happy with themselves as they are, but with themselves as they might, yet alas cannot, be."

As much as Nathan loved the drama, he never was fanatical about its place in the literary arts. Drama, indeed, is something of a conglomeration of several other arts: "It is a snatch of music, a bit of painting, a moment of dancing, a slice of sculpture, draped upon the skeleton of literature." Of course, despite this, it has an existence of its own. But it must never forget its place: "At its highest, it ranks with literature, but never above it. . . .

Drama, indeed, is dancing literature: a hybrid art." Nathan did not exclude from this belief even Shakespeare. Drama "may, at its finest as at its worst, of course, subjugate and triumph over inexperienced emotionalism, but the greatest drama of Shakespeare himself has never, in the truthful confession of cultivated emotionalism, influenced that emotionalism as has the greatest literature, or the greatest music, or the greatest painting or sculpture."

Nathan would not be Nathan, no matter what book on the theatre he wrote, if he didn't sneer at acting (in most of its manifestations) as a full-fledged art, and if he didn't excoriate most of his colleagues on the drama desk of the daily newspapers and periodicals. Most American dramatic criticism, he said, is provincial, ignorant, cowardly, "with the result that [it] is a dead art language." In his day, as now, there was a great do-to about the need for "impersonal criticism" as opposed to "personal" criticism. Nathan laughed at this. "Criticism is personal, or it is nothing. Talk to me of impersonal criticism, and I'll talk to you of impersonal sitz-bathing. Impersonal criticism is the *dodge* of the critic without personality."

The Critic and the Drama is probably Nathan's shortest book, but it is surely one of his most stimulating.

Fairleigh Dickinson University
   Rutherford, New Jersey

Of all the arts and half-arts—perhaps even above that of acting—is the art of criticism founded most greatly upon vanity. All criticism is, at bottom, an effort on the part of its practitioner to show off himself and his art at the expense of the artist and the art which he criticizes. The heavy modesty practised by certain critics is but a recognition of, and self-conscious attempt to diminish, the fundamental and ineradicable vainglory of criticism. The great critics are those who, recognizing the intrinsic, permanent and indeclinable egotism of the critical art, make no senseless effort to conceal it. The absurd critics are those who attempt to conceal it and, in the attempt, make their art and themselves doubly absurd.

I. AESTHETIC JURISPRUDENCE

I. AESTHETIC JURISPRUDENCE

A RT is a reaching out into the ugliness of the world for vagrant beauty and the imprisoning of it in a tangible dream. Criticism is the dream book. All art is a kind of subconscious madness expressed in terms of sanity; criticism is essential to the interpretation of its mysteries, for about everything truly beautiful there is ever something mysterious and disconcerting. Beauty is not always immediately recognizable as beauty; what often passes for beauty is mere infatuation; living beauty is like a love that has outlasted the middle-years of life, and has met triumphantly the test of time, and faith, and cynic meditation. For beauty is a sleep-walker in the endless corridors of the wakeful world, uncertain, groping, and not a little strange. And criticism is its tender guide.

Art is a partnership between the artist and

[3]

the artist-critic. The former creates; the latter re-creates. Without criticism, art would of course still be art, and so with its windows walled in and with its lights extinguished would the Louvre still be the Louvre. Criticism is the windows and chandeliers of art: it illuminates the enveloping darkness in which art might otherwise rest only vaguely discernible, and perhaps altogether unseen.

Criticism, at its best, is a great, tall candle on the altar of art; at its worst, which is to say in its general run, a campaign torch flaring red in behalf of æsthetic ward-heelers. This campaign torch motif in criticism, with its drunken enthusiasm and raucous hollering born of ignorance, together with what may be called the Prince Albert motif, with its sober, statue-like reserve born of ignorance that, being well-mannered, is not so bumptious as the other, has contributed largely to the common estimate of criticism as a profession but slightly more exalted than Second Avenue auctioneering if somewhat less than Fifth. Yet criticism is itself an art. It might, indeed, be well defined as an art within an art, since every work of art is the result of a struggle between the heart that is the artist himself and his mind that is the critic. Once his work is done, the artist's mind, tired from the bitterness of the struggle, takes the form of a second artist, puts on this second artist's strange hat, coat and checkered trousers, and goes forth with refreshed vigour to gossip abroad how much of the first artist's work was the result of its original splendid vitality and how much the result of its gradually diminished vitality and sad weariness. The wrangling that occurs at times between art and criticism is, at bottom, merely a fraternal discord, one in which Cain and Abel belabour each other with stuffed clubs. Criticism is often most sympathetic when it is apparently most cruel: the propounder of the sternest, hardest philosophy that the civilized world has known never failed sentimentally to kiss and embrace his sister, Therese Elisabeth Alexandra Nietzsche, every night at bed-time. "It is not possible," Cabell has written, "to draw inspiration from a woman's beauty unless you comprehend how easy it would be to murder her." And—"Only those who have firmness may be really tenderhearted," said Rochefoucauld. One may sometimes even throw mud to tonic purpose. Consider Karlsbad.

Art is the haven wherein the disillusioned may find illusion. Truth is no part of art. Nor is the mission of art simple beauty, as the text books tell us. The mission of art is the magnification of simple beauty to proportions so heroic as to be almost overpowering. Art is a gross exaggeration of natural beauty: there was never a woman so beautiful as the Venus di Milo, or a man so beautiful as the Apollo Belvedere of the Vatican, or a sky so beautiful as Monet's, or human speech so beautiful as Shakespeare's, or the song of a nightingale so beautiful as Ludwig van Beethoven's. But as art is a process of magnification, so criticism is a process of reduction. Its purpose is the reducing of the magnifications of art to the basic classic and æsthetic principles, and the subsequent announcement thereof in

[6]

terms proportioned to the artist's interplay of fundamental skill and overtopping imagination.

The most general fault of criticism lies in a confusion of its own internal processes with those of art: it is in the habit of regarding the business of art as a reduction of life to its essence of beauty, and the business of criticism as an expansion of that essence to its fullest flow. The opposite is more reasonable. Art is a beautiful, swollen lie; criticism, a cold compress. The concern of art is with beauty; the concern of criticism is with truth. And truth and beauty, despite the Sunday School, are often strangers. This confusion of the business of art and that of criticism has given birth to the so-called "contagious," or inspirational, criticism, than which nothing is more mongrel and absurd. Criticism is designed to state facts—charmingly, gracefully, if possible —but still facts. It is not designed to exhort, enlist, convert. This is the business not of the critic, but of those readers of the critic whom the facts succeed in convincing and gal-

[7]

vanizing. Contagious criticism is merely a vainglorious critic's essay at popularity: facts heated up to a degree where they melt into caressing nothingness.

But if this "criticism with a glow" is not to be given countenance, even less is to be suffered the criticism that, in its effort at a fastidious and elegant reserve, leans so far backward that it freezes its ears. This species of criticism fails not only to enkindle the reader, but fails also—and this is more important—to enkindle the critic himself. The ideal critic is perhaps much like a Thermos bottle: full of warmth, he suggests the presence of the heat within him without radiating it. This inner warmth is essential to a critic. But this inner warmth, where it exists, is automatically chilled and banished from a critic by a protracted indulgence in excessive critical reserve. Just as the professional frown assumed by a much photographed public magnifico often becomes stubbornly fixed upon his hitherto gentle brow, so does the prolonged spurious constraint of a critic in due time psychologically hoist him on his own petard. A writer's work does not grow more and more like him; a writer grows more and more like his work. The best writing that a man produces is always just a little superior to himself. There never was a literary artist who did not appreciate the difficulty of keeping up to the pace of his writings. A writer is dominated by the standard of his own writings; he is a slave *in transitu,* lashed, tormented, and miserable. The weak and inferior literary artist such a critic as the one alluded to, soon becomes the helpless victim of his own writings: like a vampire of his own creation they turn upon him and suck from him the warm blood that was erstwhile his. A pose in time becomes natural: a man with a good left eye cannot affect a monocle for years without eventually coming to need it. A critic cannot write ice without becoming in time himself at least partly frosted.

Paraphrasing Pascal, to little minds all things are great. Great art is in constant conflict with the awe of little minds. Art is something like a wonderful trapeze performer swinging high above the heads of the bewildered multitude and nervous lest it be made to lose its balance and to slip by the periodic sudden loud marvellings of the folks below. The little mind and its little criticism are the flattering foes of sound art. Such art demands for its training and triumph the countless preliminary body blows of muscular criticism guided by a muscular mind. Art and the artist cannot be developed by mere back-slapping. If art, according to Beulé, is the intervention of the human mind in the elements furnished by experience, criticism is the intervention of the human mind in the elements furnished by æsthetic passion. Art and the artist are ever youthful lovers; criticism is their chaperon.

II

I do not believe finally in this or that "theory" of criticism. There are many sound and apt species of criticism as there are works to be criticized. To say that art must be criticized only after this formula or after that, is to say that art must be contrived only out of this formula or out of that. As every work of art is an entity, a thing in itself, so is every piece of criticism an entity, a thing in itself. That "Thus Spake Zarathustra" must inevitably be criticized by the canons of the identical "theory" with which one criticizes "Tristan and Isolde" is surely difficult of reasoning.

To the Goethe-Carlyle doctrine that the critic's duty lies alone in discerning the artist's aim, his point of view and, finally, his execution of the task before him, it is easy enough to subscribe, but certainly this is not a "theory" of criticism so much as it is a foundation for a theory. To advance it as a theory, full-grown, full-fledged and flapping, as it has been advanced by the Italian Croce and his admirers, is to publish the preface to a book without the book itself. Accepted as a theory complete in itself, it fails by virtue of its several undeveloped intrinsic problems, chief among

[11]

which is its neglect to consider the undeniable fact that, though each work of art is indubitably an entity and so to be considered, there is yet in creative art what may be termed an æsthetic genealogy that bears heavily upon comprehensive criticism and that renders the artist's aim, his point of view and his execution of the task before him susceptible to a criticism predicated in a measure upon the work of the sound artist who has just preceded him.

The Goethe-Carlyle hypothesis is a little too liberal. It calls for qualifications. It gives the artist too much ground, and the critic too little. To discern the artist's aim, to discern the artist's point of view, are phrases that require an amount of plumbing, and not a few foot-notes. It is entirely possible, for example, that the immediate point of view of an artist be faulty, yet the execution of his immediate task exceedingly fine. If carefully planned triumph in art is an entity, so also may be undesigned triumph. I do not say that any such latter phenomenon is usual, but it is conceivable, and hence may be employed as a test of the critical hypothesis in point. Unschooled, without aim or point of view in the sense of this hypothesis, Schumann's compositions at the age of eleven for chorus and orchestra offer the quasi-theory some resistance. The question of the comparative merit of these compositions and the artist's subsequent work may not strictly be brought into the argument, since the point at issue is merely a theory and since theory is properly to be tested by theory.

Intent and achievement are not necessarily twins. I have always perversely thought it likely that there is often a greater degree of accident in fine art than one is permitted to believe. The aim and point of view of a bad artist are often admirable; the execution of a fine artist may sometimes be founded upon a point of view that is, from an apparently sound critical estimate, at striking odds with it. One of the finest performances in all modern dramatic writing, upon its critical reception as such, came as a great surprise to the writer who almost unwittingly had achieved it. Art is often unconscious of itself. Shakespeare, writing popular plays to order, wrote the greatest plays that dramatic art has known. Mark Twain, in a disgusted moment, threw off a practical joke, and it turned out to be literature.

A strict adherence to the principles enunciated in the Goethe-Carlyle theory would result in a confinement of art for all the theory's bold aim in exactly the opposite direction. For all the critic may accurately say, the aim and point of view of, say, Richard Strauss in "Don Quixote" and "A Hero's Life," may be imperfect, yet the one critical fact persists that the executions are remarkably fine. All things considered, it were perhaps better that the critical theory under discussion, if it be accepted at all, be turned end foremost: that the artist's execution of the task before him be considered either apart from his aim and point of view, or that it be considered first, and then—with not too much insistence upon them—his point of view and his aim. This would seem to be a more logical æsthetic and critical order. Tolstoi, with a sound, intelligent and technically perfect aim and point of view composed second-rate drama. So, too, Maeterlinck. Synge, by his own admissions adjudged critically and dramatically guilty on both counts, composed one of the truly first-rate dramas of the Anglo-Saxon stage.

In its very effort to avoid pigeon-holing, the Goethe-Carlyle theory pigeon-holes itself. In its commendable essay at catholicity, it is like a garter so elastic that it fails to hold itself up. That there may not be contradictions in the contentions here set forth, I am not sure. But I advance no fixed, definite theory of my own; I advance merely contradictions of certain of the phases of the theories held by others, and contradictions are ever in the habit of begetting contradictions. Yet such contradictions are in themselves apposite and soundly critical, since any theory susceptible of contradictions must itself be contradictory and insecure. If I suggest any theory on my

[15]

part it is a variable one: a theory that, in this instance, is one thing and in that, another. Criticism, as I see it—and I share the common opinion—is simply a sensitive, experienced and thoroughbred artist's effort to interpret, in terms of æsthetic doctrine and his own peculiar soul, the work of another artist reciprocally to that artist and thus, as with a reflecting mirror, to his public. But to state merely what criticism is, is not to state the doctrine of its application. And herein, as I see it, is where the theorists fail to cover full ground. The anatomy of criticism is composed not of one theory, but of a theory—more or less generally agreed upon—upon which are reared in turn other theories that are not so generally agreed upon. The Goethe-Carlyle theory is thus like a three-story building on which the constructor has left off work after finishing only the first story. What certain aspects of these other stories may be like, I have already tried to suggest.

I have said that, if I have any theory of my own, it is a theory susceptible in practice of numerous surface changes. These surface changes often disturb in a measure this or that phase of what lies at the bottom. Thus, speaking as a critic of the theatre, I find it impossible to reconcile myself to criticizing acting and drama from the vantage point of the same theory, say, for example, the Goethe-Carlyle theory. This theory fits criticism of drama much better than it fits criticism of acting, just as it fits criticism of painting and sculpture much more snugly than criticism of music. The means whereby the emotions are directly affected, and soundly affected, may at times be critically meretricious, yet the accomplishment itself may be, paradoxically, artistic. Perhaps the finest acting performance of our generation is Bernhardt's Camille: its final effect is tremendous: yet the means whereby it is contrived are obviously inartistic. Again, "King Lear," searched into with critical chill, is artistically a poor instance of playmaking, yet its effect is precisely the effect striven for. Surely, in cases like these, criticism founded strictly upon an inflexible theory is futile criticism, and not only futile but eminently unfair.

Here, of course, I exhibit still more contradictions, but through contradictions we may conceivably gain more secure ground. When his book is once opened, the author's mouth is shut. (Wilde, I believe, said that; and though for some peculiar reason it is today regarded as suicidal to quote the often profound Wilde in any serious argument, I risk the danger.) But when a dramatist's play or a composer's symphony is opened, the author has only begun to open his mouth. What results, an emotional art within an intellectual art, calls for a critical theory within a critical theory. To this composite end, I offer a suggestion: blend with the Goethe-Carlyle theory that of the aforementioned Wilde, to wit, that beauty is uncriticizable, since it has as many meanings as man has moods, since it is the symbol of symbols, and since it reveals everything because it expresses nothing. The trouble with criticism—again to pose a contradiction— is that, in certain instances, it is often too cerebral. Feeling a great thrill of beauty, it turns to its somewhat puzzled mind and is apprised that the thrill which it has unquestionably enjoyed from the work of art might conceivably be of pathological origin, a fremitus or vibration felt upon percussion of a hydatoid tumour.

The Goethe-Carlyle theory, properly rigid and unyielding so far as emotional groundlings are concerned, may, I believe, at times safely be chucked under the chin and offered a communication of gipsy ardour by the critic whose emotions are the residuum of trial, test and experience.

III

Coquelin put it that the footlights exaggerate everything: they modify the laws of space and of time; they put miles in a few square feet; they make minutes appear to be hours. Of this exaggeration, dramatic criticism—which is the branch of criticism of which I treat in particular—has caught something.

The Critic and the Drama

Of all the branches of criticism it is intrinsically the least sober and the least accurately balanced. It always reminds me somehow of the lash in the hands of Œacus, in "The Frogs," falling upon Bacchus and Xanthus to discover which of the two is the divine, the latter meantime endeavouring to conceal the pain that would betray their mortality by various transparent dodges. Drama is a two-souled art: half divine, half clownish. Shakespeare is the greatest dramatist who ever lived because he alone, of all dramatists, most accurately sensed the mongrel nature of his art. Criticism of drama, it follows, is similarly a two-souled art: half sober, half mad. Drama is a deliberate intoxicant; dramatic criticism, aromatic spirits of ammonia; the re-creation is never perfect; there is always a trace of tipsiness left. Even the best dramatic criticism is always just a little dramatic. It indulges, a trifle, in acting. It can never be as impersonal, however much certain of its practitioners may try, as criticism of painting or of sculpture or of literature. This is why the best criticism of the theatre must inevitably be personal criticism. The theatre itself is distinctly personal; its address is directly personal. It holds the mirror not up to nature, but to the spectator's individual idea of nature. If it doesn't, it fails. The spectator, if he is a critic, merely holds up his own mirror to the drama's mirror: a reflection of the first reflection is the result. Dramatic criticism is this second reflection. And so the best dramatic criticism has about it a flavour of the unconscious, grotesque and unpremeditated. "When Lewes was at his business," Shaw has said, "he seldom remembered that he was a gentleman or a scholar." (Shaw was speaking of Lewes' free use of vulgarity and impudence whenever they happened to be the proper tools for his job.) "In this he showed himself a true craftsman, intent on making the measurements and analyses of his criticism as accurate, and their expression as clear and vivid, as possible, instead of allowing himself to be distracted by the vanity of playing the elegant man of letters, or writing with perfect good taste, or hinting

in every line that he was above his work. In
exacting all this from himself, and taking his
revenge by expressing his most laboured con-
clusions with a levity that gave them the air
of being the unpremeditated whimsicalities of
a man who had perversely taken to writing
about the theatre for the sake of the jest
latent in his own outrageous unfitness for it,
Lewes rolled his stone up the hill quite in the
modern manner of Mr. Walkley, dissembling
its huge weight, and apparently kicking it at
random hither and thither in pure wanton-
ness."

Mr. Spingarn, in his exceptionally interesting, if somewhat overly indignant, treatise on
"Creative Criticism," provides, it seems to me,
a particularly clear illustration of the manner
in which the proponents of the more modern
theories of criticism imprison themselves in
the extravagance of their freedom. While
liberating art from all the old rules of criticism, they simultaneously confine criticism
with the new rules—or ghosts of rules—where-
with they free art. If each work of art is a

unit, a thing in itself, as is commonly agreed, why should not each work of criticism be similarly a unit, a thing in itself? If art is, in each and every case, a matter of individual expression, why should not criticism, in each and every such case, be similarly and relevantly a matter of individual expression? In freeing art of definitions, has not criticism been too severely defined? I believe that it has been. I believe that there may be as many kinds of criticism as there are kinds of art. I believe that there may be sound analytical, sound emotional, sound cerebral, sound impressionistic, sound destructive, sound constructive, and other sound species of criticism. If art knows no rules, criticism knows no rules—or, at least, none save those that are obvious. If Brahms' scherzo in E flat minor, op. 4, is an entity, a work in and of itself, why shouldn't Huneker's criticism of it be regarded as an entity, a work in and of itself? If there is in Huneker's work inspiration from without, so, too, is there in Brahms': if Brahms may be held a unit in this particular instance with no consideration of Chopin, why may not Huneker with no consideration of Brahms?

If this is pushing things pretty far, it is the Spingarns who have made the pushing necessary. "Taste," says Mr. Spingarn, "must reproduce the work of art within itself in order to understand and judge it; and at that moment æsthetic judgment becomes nothing more or less than creative art itself." This rings true. But granting the perfection of the taste, why define´ and limit the᾿ critical creative art thus born of reproduction? No sooner has a law been enunciated, writes Mr. Spingarn, than it has been broken by an artist impatient or ignorant of its restraints, and the critics have been obliged to explain away these violations of their laws or gradually to change the laws themselves. If art, he continues, is organic expression, and every work of art is to be interrogated with the question, "What has it expressed, and how completely?", there is no place for the question whether it has conformed to some convenient classification of critics or to some law derived from this classification. Once again, truly put. But so, too, no sooner have laws been enunciated than they have been broken by critics impatient or ignorant of their restraints, and the critics of critics have been obliged to explain away these violations of the laws, or gradually to change the laws themselves. And so, too, have these works of criticism provided no place for the question whether they have conformed to some convenient classification of the critics of criticism or to some law derived from this classification.

"Criticism," said Carlyle, his theories apart, "stands like an interpreter between the inspired and the uninspired, between the prophet and those who hear the melody of his words, and catch some glimpse of their material meaning, but understand not their deeper import." This is the best definition that I know of. It defines without defining; it gives into the keeping of the interpreter the hundred languages of art and merely urges him, with whatever means may best and properly suit his ends, to translate them clearly to those that do not understand; it sets him free from the very shackles which Carlyle himself, removing from art, wound in turn about him.

II. DRAMA AS AN ART

II. DRAMA AS AN ART

I

IF the best of criticism, in the familiar description of Anatole France, lies in the adventure of a soul among masterpieces, the best of drama may perhaps be described as the adventure of a masterpiece among souls. Drama is fine or impoverished in the degree that it evokes from such souls a fitting and noble reaction.

Drama is, in essence, a democratic art in constant brave conflict with aristocracy of intelligence, soul and emotion. When drama triumphs, a masterpiece like "Hamlet" comes to life. When the conflict ends in a draw, a drama half-way between greatness and littleness is the result—a drama, say, such as "El Gran Galeoto." When the struggle ends in defeat, the result is a "Way Down East" or a "Lightnin'." This, obviously, is not to say that great drama may not be popular drama, nor popular drama great drama, for I speak of drama here not as this play or that, but as a specific art. And it is as a specific art that it finds its test and trial, not in its own intrinsically democratic soul, but in the extrinsic aristocratic soul that is taste, and connoisseurship, and final judgment. Drama that has come to be at once great and popular has ever first been given the imprimatur, not of democratic souls, but of aristocratic. Shakespeare and Molière triumphed over aristocracy of intelligence, soul and emotion before that triumph was presently carried on into the domain of inferior intelligence, soul and emotion. In our own day, the drama of Hauptmann, Shaw and the American O'Neill has come into its popular own only after it first achieved the imprimatur of what we may term the unpopular, or undemocratic, theatres. Aristocracy cleared the democratic path for Ibsen, as it cleared it, in so far as possible, for Rostand and Hugo von Hofmannsthal.

Great drama is the rainbow born when the

sun of reflection and understanding smiles anew upon an intelligence and emotion which that drama has respectively shot with gleams of brilliant lightning and drenched with the rain of brilliant tears. Great drama, like great men and great women, is always just a little sad. Only idiots may be completely happy. Reflection, sympathy, wisdom, gallant gentleness, experience—the chords upon which great drama is played—these are wistful chords. The commonplace urge that drama, to be truly great, must uplift is, in the sense that the word uplift is used, childish. The mission of great drama is not to make numskulls glad that they are alive, but to make them speculate why they are permitted to be alive at all. And since this is the mission of great drama—if its mission may, indeed, be reduced to any phrase—it combines within itself, together with this mystical and awe-struck appeal to the proletariat, a direct and agreeable appeal to such persons as are, by reason of their metaphysical perception and emotional culture, superior to and contemptuous of the

[31]

proletariat. Fine drama, in truth, is usually just a trifle snobbish. It has no traffic with such souls as are readily to be made to feel "uplifted" by spurious philosophical nostrums and emotional sugar pills. Its business is with what the matchless Dryden hailed "souls of the highest rank and truest understanding": souls who find a greater uplift in the noble depressions of Brahms' first trio, Bartolommeo's Madonna della Misericordia, and Joseph Conrad's "Youth" than in the easy buoyancies of John Philip Sousa, Howard Chandler Christy and Rupert Hughes. The aim of great drama is not to make men happy with themselves as they are, but with themselves as they might, yet alas cannot, be. As Gautier has it, "The aim of art is not exact reproduction of nature, but creation, by means of forms and colours, of a microcosm wherein may be produced dreams, sensations, and ideas inspired by the aspect of the world." If drama is irrevocably a democratic art and uplift of the great masses of men its noblest end, Mrs. Porter's "Pollyanna" must endure as a work of dramatic art a thousand times finer than Corneille's "Polyeucte."

Drama has been strictly defined by the ritualists in a dozen different ways. "Drama," says one, "must be based on character, and the action proceed from character." "Drama," stipulates another, "is not an imitation of men, but of an action and of life: character is subsidiary to action." "Drama," promulgates still another, "is the struggle of a will against obstacles." And so on, so on. Rules, rules and more rules. Pigeon-holes upon pigeon-holes. Good drama is anything that interests an intelligently emotional group of persons assembled together in an illuminated hall. Molière, wise among dramatists, said as much, though in somewhat more, and doubtless too, sweeping words. Throughout the ages of drama there will be always Romanticists of one sort or another, brave and splendid spirits, who will have to free themselves from the definitions and limitations imposed upon them by the neo-Bossus and Boileaus, and the small portion Voltaires, La Harpes and Marmontels. Drama is struggle, a conflict of wills?

[33]

Then what of "Ghosts"? Drama is action? Then what of "Nachtasyl"? Drama is character? Then what of "The Dream Play"? "A 'character' upon the stage," wrote the author of the last named drama, "has become a creature ready-made—a mere mechanism that drives the man—I do not believe in these theatrical 'characters.'"

Of all the higher arts, drama is perhaps the simplest and easiest. Its anatomy is composed of all the other arts, high and low, stripped to their elementals. It is a synthesis of those portions of these other arts that, being elemental, are most easily assimilable on the part of the multitude. It is a snatch of music, a bit of painting, a moment of dancing, a slice of sculpture, draped upon the skeleton of literature. At its highest, it ranks with literature, but never above it. One small notch below, and it ranks only with itself, in its own isolated and generically peculiar field. Drama, indeed, is dancing literature: a hybrid art. It is often purple and splendid; it is often profoundly beautiful and profoundly

[34]

moving. Yet, with a direct appeal to the emotions as its first and encompassing aim, it has never, even at its finest, been able to exercise the measure of direct emotional appeal that is exercised, say, by Chopin's C sharp minor Nocturne, op. 27, No. 1, or by the soft romance of the canvases of Palma Vecchio, or by Rodin's superb "Eternal Spring," or by Zola's "La Terre." It may, at its finest as at its worst, of course subjugate and triumph over inexperienced emotionalism, but the greatest drama of Shakespeare himself has never, in the truthful confession of cultivated emotionalism, influenced that emotionalism as has the greatest literature, or the greatest music, or the greatest painting or sculpture. The splendid music of "Romeo" or "Hamlet" is not so eloquent and moving as that of "Tristan" or "Lohengrin"; no situation in the whole of Hauptmann can strike in the heart so thrilling and profound a chord of pity as a single line in Allegri's obvious "Miserere." The greatest note of comedy in drama falls short of the note of comedy in the "Coffee-

[35]

Cantata" of Bach; the greatest note of ironic remorse falls short of that in the scherzo in B minor of Chopin; the greatest intellectual note falls short of that in the first and last movements of the C minor symphony of Brahms. What play of Sudermann's has the direct appeal of "The Indian Lily"? What play made out of Hardy's "Tess," however adroitly contrived, retains the powerful appeal of the original piece of literature? To descend, what obvious thrill melodrama, designed frankly for dollars, has—with all its painstaking and deliberate intent—yet succeeded in provoking half the thrill and shock of the obvious second chapter of Andreas Latzko's equally obvious "Men in War"?

Art is an evocation of beautiful emotions: art is art in the degree that it succeeds in this evocation: drama succeeds in an inferior degree. Whatever emotion drama may succeed brilliantly in evoking, another art succeeds in evoking more brilliantly.

II

Although, of course, one speaks of drama here primarily in the sense of acted drama, it is perhaps not necessary so strictly to confine one's self. For when the critic confines himself in his discussion of drama to the acted drama, he regularly brings upon himself from other critics—chiefly bookish fellows whose theatrical knowledge is meagre—the very largely unwarranted embarrassment of arguments anent "crowd psychology" and the like which, while they have little or nothing to do with the case, none the less make a certain deep impression upon his readers. (Readers of criticism become automatically critics; with his first sentence, the critic challenges his critic-reader's sense of argument.) This constantly advanced contention of "crowd psychology," of which drama is supposed to be at once master and slave, has small place in a consideration of drama, from whatever sound point of view one elects to consider the latter. If "crowd psychology" operates in the case of

[37]

theatre drama, it operates also in the case of concert-hall music. Yet no one so far as I know seriously maintains that, in a criticism of music, this "crowd psychology" has any place.

I have once before pointed out that, even accepting the theory of crowd psychology and its direct and indirect implications so far as drama is concerned, it is as nonsensical to assume that one thousand persons assembled together before a drama in a theatre are, by reason of their constituting a crowd, any more likely to be moved automatically than the same crowd of one thousand persons assembled together before a painting in an art gallery. Furthermore, the theory that collective intelligence and emotionalism are a more facile and ingenuous intelligence and emotionalism, while it may hold full water in the psychological laboratory, holds little in actual external demonstration, particularly in any consideration of a crowd before one of the arts. While it may be true that the Le Bon and Tarde theory applies aptly to the collective psychology of a crowd at a prize-fight or a bull-fight or

a circus, one may be permitted severe doubts
that it holds equally true of a crowd in a
theatre or in an art gallery or in a concert hall.
The tendency of such a latter group is not
æsthetically downward, but upward. And
not only æsthetically, but intellectually and
emotionally. (I speak, of course, and with
proper relevance, of a crowd assembled to hear
good drama or good music, or to see good
painting. The customary obscuring tactic of
critics in this situation is to argue out the principles of intelligent reaction to good drama in
terms of yokel reaction to bad drama. Analy-
sis of the principles of sound theatre drama
and the reaction of a group of eight hundred
citizens of Marion, Ohio, to "The Two Or-
phans" somehow do not seem to me to be
especially apposite.) The fine drama or the
fine piece of music does not make its auditor
part of a crowd; it removes him, and every
one else in the crowd, from the crowd, and
makes him an individual. The crowd ceases
to exist as a crowd; it becomes a crowd of
units, of separate individuals. The dramas of

Mr. Owen Davis make crowds; the dramas of Shakespeare make individuals.

The argument to the contrary always somewhat grotesquely assumes that the crowd assembled at a fine play, and promptly susceptible to group psychology, is a new crowd, one that has never attended a fine play before. Such an assumption falls to pieces in two ways. Firstly, it is beyond reason to believe that it is true in more than one instance out of a hundred; and secondly it would not be true even if it were true. For, granting that a crowd of one thousand persons were seeing great drama for the first time in their lives, what reason is there for believing that the majority of persons in the crowd who had never seen great drama and didn't know exactly what to make of it would be swayed and influenced by the minority who had never seen great drama but did know what to make of it? If this were true, no great drama could ever possibly fail in the commercial theatre. Or, to test the hypothesis further, take it the other way round. What reason is there for believing that the majority in this crowd would be moved the one way or the other, either by a minority that did understand the play, or did not understand it? Or take it in another way still. What reason is there for believing that the minority in this crowd who did know what the drama was about would be persuaded emotionally by the majority who did not know what the drama was about?

Theories, and again theories. But the facts fail to support them. Take the lowest type of crowd imaginable, one in which there is not one cultured man in a thousand—the crowd, say, at a professional American baseball game —and pack it into an American equivalent for Reinhardt's Grosses Schauspielhaus. The play, let us say, is "Œdipus Rex." At the ball game, the crowd psychology of Le Bon operated to the full. But what now? Would the crowd, in the theatre and before a great drama, be the same crowd? Would it not be an entirely different crowd? Would not its group psychology promptly and violently suffer a sudden change? Whether out of curios-

ity, disgust, admiration, social shame or what
not, would it not rapidly segregate itself,
spiritually or physically, into various groups?
What is the Le Bon theatrical view of the
crowd psychology that somehow didn't come
off during the initial engagement of Barrie's
"Peter Pan" in Washington, D. C.? Or of
the crowd psychology that worked the other
way round when Ibsen was first played in London? Or of the crowd psychology that, operating regularly, if artificially, at the New
York premières, most often fails, for all its
high enthusiasm, to move either the minority
or the majority in its composition?

The question of sound drama and the pack
psychology of a congress of groundlings is a
fatuous one: it gets nowhere. Sound drama
and sound audiences are alone to be considered
at one and the same time. And, as I have
noted, the tendency of willing, or even semi-
willing, auditors and spectators is in an upward direction, not a downward. No intelligent spectator at a performance of "Ben Hur"
has ever been made to feel like throwing his

hat into the air and cheering by the similar actions of the mob spectators to the left and right of him. No ignoble auditor of "The Laughter of the Gods" but has been made to feel, in some part, the contagion of cultivated appreciation to *his* left and right. "I forget," wrote Sarcey, in a consideration of the subject of which we have been treating, "what tyrant it was of ancient Greece to whom massacres were everyday affairs, but who wept copiously over the misfortunes of a heroine in a tragedy. He was the audience; and for the one evening clothed himself in the sentiments of the public." A typical example of sophisticated reasoning. How does Sarcey know that it was not the rest of the audience—the crowd—that was influenced by this repentant and copiously lachrymose individual, rather than that it was this individual who was moved by the crowd?

If fallacies perchance insinuate themselves into these opposing contentions, it is a case of fallacy versus fallacy: my intent is not so much to prove anything as to indicate the presence of holes in the proofs of the other side. These holes seem to me to be numerous, and of considerable circumference. A description of two of them may suffice to suggest the rest. Take, as the first of these, the familar Castelvetro doctrine that, since a theatrical audience is not a select congress but a motley crowd, the dramatist, ever conscious of the group psychology, must inevitably avoid all themes and ideas unintelligible to such a gathering. It may be true that a theatrical audience is not a select congress, but why confine the argument to theatrical audiences and seek thus to prove something of drama that may be proved as well—if one is given to such idiosyncrasies—of music? What, as I have said before, of opera and concert hall audiences? Consider the average audience at Covent Garden, the Metropolitan, Carnegie Hall. Is it any way culturally superior to the average audience at the St. James's Theatre, or the Théâtre de l'Oeuvre, or the Plymouth—or even the Neighbourhood Playhouse down in Grand Street? What of the audiences who attended the original performances of Beethoven's "Leonore" ("Fidelio"), Berlioz's "Benvenuto Cellini," the original performances of Wagner in France and the performances of his "Der Flie-gende Holländer" in Germany, the operas of Händel in England in the years 1733–37, the work of Rossini in Italy, the concerts of Chopin during his tour of England and Scotland? . . . Again, as to the imperative necessity of the dramatist's avoidance of all themes and ideas unintelligible to a mob audience, what of the success among such very audiences of—to name but a few more recent profitably produced and locally readily recognizable examples—Shaw's "Getting Married," Augustus Thomas' "The Witching Hour," Ibsen's "The Wild Duck," Dunsany's "The Laughter of the Gods," Barrie's "Mary Rose," Strindberg's "The Father," Synge's "Playboy"? . . . Surely it will be quickly allowed that however obvious the themes and ideas of these plays may be to the few, they are hardly within the ready intelligence of what the theorists picture as the imaginary mob theatre audience. Fine drama is independent of all such theories: the dramatist who subscribes to them should not figure in any treatise upon drama as an art.

A second illustration: the equivocation to the effect that drama, being a democratic art, may not properly be evaluated in terms of more limited, and aristocratic, taste. It seems to me, at least, an idiotic assumption that drama is a more democratic art than music. All great art is democratic in intention, if not in reward. Michelangelo, Shakespeare, Wagner and Zola are democratic artists, and their art democratic art. It is criticism of Michelangelo, Shakespeare, Wagner and Zola that is aristocratic. Criticism, not art, generically wears the ermine and the purple. To appraise a democratic art in terms of democracy is to attempt to effect a chemical reaction in nitrogen with nitrogen. If drama is, critically, a democratic art since it is meant not to be read by the few but to be played before the many, music must be critically no less a democratic art. Yet the theorists conveniently overlook this embarrassment. Nevertheless, if Shakespeare's dramas were designed for the heterogeneous ear, so, too, were the songs of Schumann. No great artist has ever in his heart deliberately fashioned his work for a remote and forgotten cellar, dark and stairless. He fashions it, for all his doubts, in the hope of hospitable eyes and ears, and in the hope of a sun to shine upon it. It is as ridiculous to argue that because Shakespeare's is a democratic art it must be criticized in terms of democratic reaction to it as it would be to argue that because the United States is a democracy the most acute and comprehensive criticism of that democracy must lie in a native democrat's reaction to it. "To say that the theatre is for the people," says Gordon Craig, "is necessary. But to forget to add that part and parcel of the people is the aristocracy, whether of birth or feeling, is an omission. A man of the eighteenth century, dressed in silks, in a fashionable loggia in the theatre at Versailles, looking as if he did no work (as Voltaire in his youth may have looked), presents, in essence, exactly the same picture as Walt Whitman in his rough gray suit lounging in the Bowery, also looking as if he did no work. . . . One the aristocrat, one the democrat: the two are identical."

III

"Convictions," said Nietzsche, "are prisons." Critical "theories," with negligible exception, seek to denude the arts of their splendid, gipsy gauds and to force them instead to don so many duplicated black and white striped uniforms. Of all the arts, drama has suffered most in this regard. Its critics, from the time of Aristotle, have bound and fettered it, and have then urged it impassionedly to soar. Yet, despite its shackles, it has triumphed, and each triumph has been a derision of one of its most famous and distinguished critics. It triumphed, through Shakespeare, over Aristotle; it triumphed, through Molière, over Castelvetro; it triumphed, through Lemercier, over Diderot; it triumphed, through Lessing,

[48]

over Voltaire; it triumphed, through Ibsen, over Flaubert; it has triumphed, through Hauptmann, over Sarcey and, through Schnitzler and Bernard Shaw, over Mr. Archer. The truth perhaps is that drama is an art as flexible as the imaginations of its audiences. It is no more to be bound by rules and theories than such imaginations are to be bound by rules and theories. Who so all-wise that he may say by what rules or set of rules living imaginations and imaginations yet unborn are to be fanned into theatrical flame? "Imagination," Samuel Johnson's words apply to auditor as to artist, "a licentious and vagrant faculty, unsusceptible of limitations and impatient of restraint, has always endeavoured to baffle the logician, to perplex the confines of distinction, and burst the inclosures of regularity." And further, "There is therefore scarcely any species of writing of which we can tell what is its essence, and what are its constituents; every new genius produces some innovation which, when invented and approved, subverts the rules which the practice of foregoing authors had established."

Does the play interest, and whom? This seems to me to be the only doctrine of dramatic criticism that is capable of supporting itself soundly. First, does the play interest? In other words, how far has the dramatist succeeded in expressing himself, and the materials before him, intelligently, eloquently, symmetrically, beautifully? So much for the criticism of the dramatist as an artist. In the second place, whom does the play interest? Does it interest inferior persons, or does it interest cultivated and artistically sensitive persons? So much for the criticism of the artist as a dramatist.

The major difficulty with critics of the drama has always been that, having once positively enunciated their critical credos, they have been constrained to devote their entire subsequent enterprise and ingenuity to defending the fallacies therein. Since a considerable number of these critics have been, and are, extraordinarily shrewd and ingenious men, these defences of error have often been con-

trived with such persuasive dexterity and reasonableness that they have endured beyond the
more sound doctrines of less deft critics, doctrines which, being sound, have suffered the
rebuffs that gaunt, grim logic, ever unprepos-
sessing and unhypnotic, suffers always. "I
hope that I am right; if I am not right, I am
still right," said Brunetière. "Mr. William
Archer is not only, like myself, a convinced,
inflexible determinist," Henry Arthur Jones
has written, "I am persuaded that he is also,
unlike myself, a consistent one. I am sure he
takes care that his practice agrees with his
opinions—even when they are wrong." Dramatic criticism is an attempt to formulate rules
of conduct for the lovable, wayward, charming,
wilful vagabond that is the drama. For the
drama is an art with a feather in its cap and
an ironic smile upon its lips, sauntering impu-
dently over forbidden lawns and through
closed lanes into the hearts of those of us
children of the world who have never grown
up. Beside literature, it is the Mother Goose
of the arts: a gorgeous and empurpled Mother

Goose for the fireside of impressible and romantic youth that, looking upward, leans ever hushed and expectant at the knee of life. It is a fairy tale told realistically, a true story told as romance. It is the lullaby of disillusion, the chimes without the cathedral, the fears and hopes and dreams and passions of those who cannot fully fear and hope and dream and flame of themselves.

"The drama must have reality," so Mr. P. P. Howe in his engaging volume of "Dramatic Portraits," "but the first essential to our understanding of an art is that we should not believe it to be actual life. The spectator who shouts his warning and advice to the heroine when the villain is approaching is, in the theatre, the only true believer in the hand of God; and he is liable to find it in a drama lower than the best." The art of the drama is one which imposes upon drama the obligation of depicting at once the inner processes of life realistically, and the external aspects of life delusively. Properly and sympathetically to appreciate drama, one must look upon it synchro-

nously with two different eyes: the one argu-
ing against the other as to the truth of what it
sees, and triumphing over this doubtful other
with the full force of its sophistry.   Again inevitably to quote Coleridge, "Stage presenta-
tions are to produce a sort of temporary half-
faith, which the spectator encourages in himself and supports by a voluntary contribution
on his own part, because he knows that it is
at all times in his power to see the thing as it
really is.   Thus the true stage illusion as to a
forest scene consists, not in the mind's judging
it to be a forest, but in its remission of the
judgment that it is not a forest."   This obviously applies to drama as well as to dramatic investiture.   One never for a moment
believes absolutely that Mr. John Barrymore
is Richard III; one merely agrees, for the
sake of Shakespeare, who has written the play,
and Mr. Hopkins, who has cast it, that Mr.
John Barrymore is Richard III, that one may
receive the ocular, aural and mental sensations for which one has paid three dollars and
a half.   Nor does one for a moment believe

that Mr. Walter Hampden, whom that very
evening one has seen dividing a brobdingna-
gian dish of goulash with Mr. Oliver Herford
in the Player's Club and discussing the pros-
pects of the White Sox, is actually speaking
extemporaneously the rare verbal embroider-
ies of Shakespeare; or that Miss Ethel Barrymore who is billed in front of Browne's Chop
House to take a star part in the Actors'
Equity Association's benefit, is really the
queen of a distant kingdom.

The dramatist, in the theatre, is not a
worker in actualities, but in the essence of actualities that filters through the self-decep-
tion of his spectators. There is no such thing
as realism in the theatre: there is only mimicry of realism. There is no such thing as
romance in the theatre: there is only mimicry
of romance. There is no such thing as
an automatic dramatic susceptibility in a theatre audience: there is only a volitional dramatic susceptibility. Thus, it is absurd to
speak of the drama holding the mirror up to
nature; all that the drama can do is to hold

[54]

nature up to its own peculiar mirror which, like that in a pleasure-park carousel, amusingly fattens up nature, or shrinks it, yet does not at any time render it unrecognizable. One does not go to the theatre to see life and nature; one goes to see the particular way in which life and nature happen to look to a cultivated, imaginative and entertaining man who happens, in turn, to be a playwright. Drama is the surprising pulling of a perfectly obvious, every-day rabbit out of a perfectly obvious, every-day silk hat. The spectator has seen thousands of rabbits and thousands of silk hats, but he has never seen a silk hat that had a rabbit concealed in it, and he is curious about it.

But if drama is essentially mimetic, so also —as Professor Gilbert Murray implies—is criticism essentially mimetic in that it is representative of the work criticized. It is conceivable that one may criticize Mr. Ziegfeld's "Follies" in terms of the "Philoctetes" of Theodectes—I myself have been guilty of even more exceptional feats; it is not only conceivable, but of common occurrence, for certain of our academic American critics to criticize the plays of Mr. Shaw in terms of Scribe and Sardou, and with a perfectly straight face; but criticism in general is a chameleon that takes on something of the colour of the pattern upon which it imposes itself. There is drama in Horace's "Epistola ad Pisones," a criticism of drama. There is the spirit of comedy in Hazlitt's essay "On the Comic Writers of the Last Century." Dryden's "Essay on Dramatic Poesy" is poetry. There is something of the music of Chopin in Huneker's critical essays on Chopin, and some of Mary Garden's spectacular histrionism in his essay on her acting. Walkley, criticizing "L'Enfant Prodigue," uses the pen of Pierrot. Criticism, more than drama with her mirror toward nature, holds the mirror up to the nature of the work it criticizes. Its end is the revivification of the passion of art which has been spent in its behalf, but under the terms laid down by Plato. Its aim is to reconstruct a great work of art on a diminutive scale, that eyes which are not capable of gazing on high may have it within the reach of their vision. Its aim is to play again all the full richness of the artist's emotional organ tones, in so far as is possible, on the cold cerebral xylophone that is criticism's deficient instrument. In the accomplishment of these aims, it is bound by no laws that art is not bound by. There is but one rule: there are no rules. Art laughs at locksmiths.

It has been a favourite diversion of critics since Aristotle's day to argue that drama is drama, whether one reads it from a printed page or sees it enacted in a theatre. Great drama, they announce, is great drama whether it ever be acted or not; "it speaks with the same voice in solitude as in crowds"; and "all the more then"—again I quote Mr. Spingarn —"will the drama itself 'even apart from representation and actors,' as old Aristotle puts it, speak with its highest power to the imagination fitted to understand and receive it." Upon this point of view much of the academic criticism of drama has been based.

But may we not well reply that, for all the fact that Shakespeare would still be the greatest dramatist who ever lived had he never been played in the theatre, so, too, would Bach still be the greatest composer who ever lived had his compositions never been played at all? If drama is not meant for actors, may we not also argue that music is not meant for instruments? Are not such expedients less sound criticism than clever evasion of sound criticism: a frolicsome and agreeable straddling of the æsthetic see-saw? There is the printed drama—criticize it. There is the same drama acted—criticize it. Why quibble? Sometimes, as in the case of "Gioconda" and Duse, they are one. Well and good. Sometimes, as in the case of "Chantecler" and Maude Adams, they are not one. Well and good. But where, in either case, the confusion that the critics lay such stress upon? These critics deal not with theories, but with mere words. They take two dozen empty words and adroitly seek therewith to fashion a fecund theory. The result is—

words. "Words which," said Ruskin, "if they are not watched, will do deadly work sometimes. There are masked words droning and skulking about us just now . . . (there never were so many, owing to the teaching of catechisms and phrases at school instead of human meanings) . . . there never were creatures of prey so mischievous, never diplomatists so cunning, never poisoners so deadly, as these masked words: they are the unjust stewards of men's ideas. . . ."

III. THE PLACE OF THE THEATRE

III. THE PLACE OF THE THEATRE

I

THE theatre stands in relation to drama much as the art gallery stands in relation to painting.   Its aim is to set off drama in such surroundings and in such light as to bring it within the comfortable vision and agreeable scrutiny of the nomad public.   To say that fine drama may produce an equal effect read as acted may be true or not as you choose, but so too a fine painting may produce an equal effect beheld in one's library as in the Uffizi.   Art thrives—art leads to art—on sympathy and a measure of general understanding.   Otherwise, of what use criticism? To divorce the theatre from a consideration of drama as an art, to contend, as it has been contended from Aristotle's day to Corneille's, and from Dryden's and Lamb's to our own,

[63]

that "the more lasting and noble design" of drama rests in a reading rather than a seeing, may be, strictly, a logical æsthetic manœuvre, but equally a logical æsthetic manœuvre would be a divorcement of canvas from painting as an art. The theatre is the canvas of drama. The printed drama is like a bubbling and sunlit spring, encountered only by wanderers into the hills and awaiting the bottling process of the theatre to carry its tonic waters far and wide among an expectant and emotionally ill people.

The criticism that nominates itself to hold drama and the theatre as things apart is a criticism which, for all its probable integrity and reason, suffers from an excessive aristocracy, like a duchess in a play by Mr. Sydney Grundy. Its æsthetic nose is elevated to such a degree that it may no longer serve as a practical organ of earthly smell, but merely as a quasi-wax feature to round out the symmetry of the face. It is criticism in a stiff corset, erect, immobile, lordly—like the Prussian lieutenant of yesterday, a striking figure, yet just a little absurd. It is sound, but like many things that are sound in æsthetics, it has its weak points, even its confounding points. For they say that propaganda can have no place in art, and along comes a Hauptmann and writes a "Weavers." Or they say that art is form, and along comes a Richard Strauss and composes two songs for baritone and orchestra that set the critics to a mad chasing of their own tails. Or, opposing criticism as an art, they say that "criticism is art in form, but its content is judgment, which takes it out of the intuitional world into the conceptual world"— and along comes an H. G. Wells with his "The New Machiavelli" which, like criticism, is art in form and its content judgment. To hold that the drama as an art may achieve its highest end read by the individual and not acted in the theatre, is to hold that music as an art may achieve its highest end played by but one instrument and not by an orchestra. The theatre is the drama's orchestra: upon the wood of its boards and the wind of its puppets is the melody of drama in all its full richness

[65]

sounded. What if drama is art and the theatre not art? What if "Hamlet" is art and electric lights and cheese-cloth are not art? Schubert's piano trio, op. 99, is art, and a pianoforte is a mere wooden box containing a number of little hammers that hit an equal number of steel and copper wires. What if I can read a full imagination into "Romeo and Juliet" and thus people it and make it live for me, without going to the theatre? So, too, can I read a full melody into the manuscript of a song by Hugo Wolf and thus make it sing for me, without going to a concert hall. But why? Is there only one way to appreciate and enjoy art—and since when? Wagner on a single violin is Wagner; Wagner on all the orchestra is super-Wagner. To read a great drama is to play "Parsifal" on a cornet and an oboe.

The object of the theatre is not, as is habitually maintained, a shrewd excitation of the imagination of a crowd, but rather a shrewd relaxation of that imagination. It is a faulty axiom that holds the greatest actor in the theatre to be an audience's imagination, and the adroit cultivation of the latter to be ever productive of large financial return. As I have on more than one occasion pointed out from available and acutely relevant statistics, the more a dramatist relies upon the imagination of an audience, the less the box-office reward that is his. An audience fills a theatre auditorium not so eager to perform with its imagination as to have its imagination performed upon. This is not the paradox it may superficially seem to be. The difference is the difference between a prompt commercial failure like Molnar's "Der Gardeofficier" ("Where Ignorance Is Bliss") which asks an audience to perform with its imagination and a great commercial success like Barrie's "Peter Pan" which performs upon the audience's imagination by supplying to it every detail of imagination, ready-made and persuasively labelled. The theatre is not a place to which one goes in search of the unexplored corners of one's imagination; it is a place to which one goes in repeated search of the familiar corners of one's imagination. The moment the dramatist works in the direction of unfamiliar corners, he is lost. This, contradictorily enough, is granted by the very critics who hold to the imagination fallacy which I have just described. They unanimously agree that a dramatist's most successful cultivation of an audience lies in what they term, and nicely, the mood of recognition, and in the same breath paradoxically contend that sudden imaginative shock is a desideratum no less.

In this pleasant remission of the active imagination lies one of the secrets of the charm of the theatre. Nor is the theatre alone in this. On even the higher plane of the authentic arts a measure of the same phenomenon assists in what may perhaps not too far-fetchedly be termed the negative stimulation of the spectator's fancy. For all the pretty and winning words to the contrary, no person capable of sound introspection will admit that a beautiful painting like Giorgione's "The Concert" or a beautiful piece of sculpture like Pisano's Perugian fountain actually and literally stirs his imagination, and sets it a-sail across hitherto uncharted æsthetic seas. What such a painting or piece of sculpture does is to reach out and, with its overpowering beauty, encompass and æsthetically fence in the antecedent wandering and uncertain imagination of its spectator. As in the instance of drama, it does not so much awaken a dormant imagination as soothe an imagination already awake. Of all the arts, music alone remains a telegrapher of unborn dreams.

The theatre brings to the art of drama concrete movement, concrete colour, and concrete final effectiveness: this, in all save a few minor particulars. The art of drama suffers, true enough, when the theatre, even at its finest, is challenged by it to produce the values intrinsic in its ghost of a dead king, or in its battle on Bosworth Field, or in its ship torn by the tempest, or in its fairy wood on midsummer night, or in its approaching tread of doom of the gods of the mountain. But for each such defeat it prospers doubly in the gifts that the theatre brings to it. Such gifts as the leader

Craig has brought to the furtherance of the beauty of "Electra" and "Hamlet," as Reinhardt and his aides have brought to "Ariadne" and "Julius Cæsar," as Golovine and Appia and Bakst and Linnebach and half a dozen others have brought to the classics that have called to them, are not small ones. They have crystallized the glory of drama, have taken so many loose jewels and given them substantial and appropriate settings which have fittingly posed their radiance. To say that the reading imagination of the average cultured man is superior in power of suggestion and depiction to the imagination of the theatre is idiotically to say that the reading imagination of every average cultured man is superior in these powers to the combined theatrical imaginations of Gordon Craig, Max Reinhardt and Eleanora Duse operating jointly upon the same play. Even a commonplace imagination can successfully conjure up a landscape more beautiful than any painted by Poussin or Gainsborough, or jewels more opalescent than any painted by Rembrandt, or a woman's dress more luminous than any painted by Fortuny, or nymphs more beguiling than any of Rubens', yet who so foolish to say—as they are wont foolishly to say of reading imagination and the drama—that such an imagination is therefore superior to that of the artists? This, in essence, is none the less the serious contention of those who decline to reconcile themselves to the theatrically produced drama. This contention, reduced to its skeleton, is that, since the vice-president of the Corn Exchange Bank can picture the chamber in the outbuilding adjoining Gloster's castle more greatly to his satisfaction than Adolphe Appia can picture it for him on the stage, the mental performance of the former is therefore a finer artistic achievement than the stage performance of the latter.

II

The word imagination leads critics to queer antics. It is, perhaps, the most manhandled word in our critical vocabulary. It is used almost invariably in its literal meaning: no shades and shadows are vouchsafed to it. Imagination, in good truth, is not the basis of art, but an overtone. Many an inferior artist has a greater imagination than many a superior artist. Maeterlinck's imagination is much richer than Hauptmann's, Erik Satie's is much richer than César Franck's, and I am not at all certain that Romain Rolland's is not twice as opulent as Thomas Hardy's. Imagination is the slave of the true artist, the master of the weak. The true artist beats imagination with the cat-o'-nine-tails of his individual technic until it cries out in pain, and this pain is the work of art which is born. The inferior craftsman comfortably confounds imagination with the finished work, and so pets and coddles it; and imagination's resultant mincings and giggles he then vaingloriously sets forth as resolute art.

The theatre offers to supplement, embroider and enrich the imagination of the reader of drama with the imaginations of the actor, the scene designer, the musician, the costumer and the producing director. Each of these, before he sets himself to his concrete task, has—like the lay reader—sought the fruits of his own reading imagination. The fruits of these five reading imaginations are then assembled, carefully assorted, and the most worthy of them deftly burbanked. The final staging of the drama is merely a staging of these best fruits of the various reading imaginations. To say, against this, that it is most often impossible to render a reading imagination into satisfactory concrete forms is doubtless to say what is, strictly, true. But art itself is at its highest merely an approach toward limitless imagination and beauty. Æsthetics is a pilgrim on the road to a Mecca that is ever just over the sky-line. Of how many great works of art can one say, with complete and final conviction, that art in this particular direction can conceivably go no farther? Is it not conceivable that some super-Michelangelo will some day fashion an even more perfect "Slave," and some super-Shakespeare an even more beautiful poetic drama?

The Critic and the Drama

The detractors of the theatre are often expert in persuasive half-truths and masters of dialectic sleight-of-hand. Their performances are often so adroit that the spectator is quick to believe that the trunk is really empty, yet the false bottom is there for all its cunning concealment. Take, for example, George Moore, in the preface to his last play, "The Coming of Gabrielle." "The illusion created by externals, scenes, costumes, lighting and short sentences is in itself illusory," he professes to believe, though why he numbers the dramatist's short sentences among the externals of the stage is not quite clear. "The best performances of plays and operas are witnessed at rehearsals. Jean de Reszke was never so like Tristan at night as he was in the afternoon when he sang the part in a short jacket, a bowler hat and an umbrella in his hand. The chain armour and the plumes that he wore at night were but a distraction, setting our thoughts on periods, on the short swords in use in the ninth century in Ireland or in Cornwall, on the comfort or the discomfort of

the ships in which the lovers were voyaging,
on the absurd night-dress which is the convention that Isolde should appear in, a garment
she never wore and which we know to be make-
believe. But the hat and feathers that Isolde
appears in when she rehearses the part are
forgotten the moment she sings; and if I had
to choose to see Forbes-Robertson play Hamlet or rehearse Hamlet, I should not hesitate
for a moment. The moment he speaks he
ceases to be a modern man, but in black hose
the illusion ceases, for we forget the Prince
of Denmark and remember the mummer."
Years ago, in a volume of critical essays given
the title "Another Book on the Theatre," I
took a boyish delight in setting off precisely
the same noisy firework just to hear the folks
in the piazza rocking-chairs let out a yell.
These half-truths serve criticism as sauce
serves asparagus: they give tang to what is
otherwise often tasteless food. This is particularly true with criticism at its most geomet-
rical and profound, since such criticism, save
in rare instances, is not especially lively read-

ing. But, nevertheless, the sauce is not the
asparagus. And when Mr. Moore (doubtless with his tongue in his cheek) observes that
he can much more readily imagine the lusty
Frau Tillie Pfirsich-Melba as Isolde in a pink
and green ostrich feather hat confected in
some Friedrichstrasse atelier than in the customary stage trappings, he allows, by implication, that he might even more readily imagine
the elephantine lady as the seductive Carmen
if she had no clothes on at all.

This is the trouble with paradoxes. It is
not that they prove too little, as is believed
of them, but that they prove altogether too
much. If the illusion created by stage externals is in itself illusory, as Mr. Moore says, the
complete deletion of all such stage externals
should be the best means for providing absolute illusion. Yet the complete absence of illusion where this is the case is all too familiar
to any of us who have looked on such specta-
cles as "The Bath of Phryne" and the like in
the theatres of Paris. A prodigality of stage
externals does not contribute to disillusion,

but to illusion. These externals have become, through protracted usage, so familiar that they are, so to speak, scarcely seen: they are taken by the eye for granted. By way of proof, one need only consider two types of Shakespearian production, one like that of Mr. Robert Mantell and one like that lately employed for "Macbeth" by Mr. Arthur Hopkins. Where the overladen stereotyped first production paradoxically fades out of the picture for the spectator and leaves the path of illusion clear for him, the superlatively simple second production, almost wholly bereft of familiar externals, arrests and fixes his attention and makes illusion impossible. It is true, of course, that all this may be changed in time, when the deletion of externals by the new stagecraft shall have become a convention of the theatre as the heavy laying-on of externals is a convention at present. But, as things are today, these externals are, negatively, the most positive contributors to illusion.

It is the misfortune of the theatre that

critics have almost always approached it, and
entered it, with a defiant and challenging air.
I have, during the eighteen years of my active
critical service, met with and come to know at
least fifty professional critics in America, in
England and on the Continent, and among all
this number there have been but four who have
approached the theatre enthusiastically prejudiced in its favour—two of them asses.
But between the one large group that has been
critically hostile and the other smaller group
that has been uncritically effervescent, I have
encountered no sign of calm and reasoned
compromise, no sign of frank and intelligent
willingness to regard each and every theatre
as a unit, and so to be appraised, instead of
lumping together good and bad theatres alike
and labelling the heterogeneous mass "the
theatre." There is no such thing as "the
theatre." There is this theatre, that theatre,
and still that other theatre. Each is a unit.
To talk of "the theatre" is to talk of the Greek
theatre, the Elizabethan theatre and the modern theatre in one breath, or to speak simul-

taneously of the Grosses Schauspielhaus of Max Reinhardt and the Eltinge Theatre of Mr. A. H. Woods. "The theatre," of course, has certain more or less minor constant and enduring conventions—at least, so it seems as far as we now can tell—but so, too, has chirography, yet we do not speak of "the chirography." There are some theatres—I use the word in its proper restricted sense—that glorify drama and enhance its beauty; there are others that vitiate drama. But so also are there some men who write fine drama, and others who debase drama to mere fodder for witlings. . . . The Shakespeare of the theatre of Gordon Craig is vivid and brilliant beauty. Call it art or not art as you will—what does a label matter? The Molière of the theatre of Alexander Golovine is suggestive and exquisite enchantment. Call it art or not art as you will—what does a label matter? The Wagner of the opera house of Ludwig Sievert is triumphant and rapturous splendour. Call it anything you like—and again, what does a label matter? There are too many labels in the world.

IV. THE PLACE OF ACTING

IV. THE PLACE OF ACTING

I

"WHEN Mr. Nathan says that acting is not an art, of course he is talking arrant rot—who could doubt it, after witnessing a performance by the great Duse?" So, the estimable actor, Mr. Arnold Daly. Whether acting is or is not an art, it is not my concern at the moment to consider, yet I quote the *riposte* of Mr. Daly as perhaps typical of those who set themselves as defenders of the yea theory. It seems to me that if this is a satisfactory *touche* no less satisfactory should be some such like rejoinder as: "When Mr. Nathan says that acting *is* an art, of course he is talking arrant rot—who could doubt it, after witnessing a performance by Mr. Corse Payton."

If an authentic art is anything which may properly be founded upon an exceptionally

[83]

brilliant performance, then, by virtue of the
Reverend Doctor Ernest M. Stires' brilliant
performance in it, is pulpiteering an art, and,
on the strength of Miss Bird Millman's brilliant performance in it, is tight-rope walking
an art no less. Superficially a mere dialectic
monkey-trick, this is yet perhaps not so absurd
as it may seem, for if Duse's art lies in the
fact that she breathes life and dynamic effect
into the written word of the artist D'Annunzio, Stires' lies in the more substantial fact
that he breathes life and dynamic effect into
the word of the somewhat greater, and more
evasive artist, God. And Miss Millman, too,
brings to her quasi-art, movement, colour,
rhythm, beauty and—one may even say—a
sense of fantastic character, since the effect
she contrives is less that of a dumpy little
woman in a short white skirt pirouetting on a
taut wire than of an unreal creature, half bird,
half woman, out of some forgotten fable.

The circumstance that Duse is an artist
who happens to be an actress does not make
acting an art any more than the circumstance

that Villon was an artist who happened to be
a burglar or that Paderewski is an artist who
happens to be a politician makes burglary and
politics arts.   Duse is an artist first, and an
actress second: one need only look into her
very great share in the creation of the dramas
bearing the name of D'Annunzio to reconcile
one's self—if not too stubborn, at least in part
—to this point of view.   So, also, were
Clairon, Rachel and Jane Hading artists
apart from histrionism, and so too, is Sarah
Bernhardt: who can fail to detect the creative
artist in the "Mémoires" of the first named, for
instance, or, in the case of the last named, in
the fertile impulses of her essays in sculpture,
painting and dramatic literature?   It is a curious thing that, in all the pronouncements of
acting as an art, the names chosen by the advo-
cates as representative carriers of the æsthetic
banner are those of actors and actresses who
have most often offered evidence of artistic
passion in fields separate and apart from their
histrionic   endeavours.   Lemaître,   Salvini,
Rachel, Talma, Coquelin, Betterton, Garrick,

Fanny Kemble, the Bancrofts, Irving, Tree, and on down—far down—the line to Ditrich-stein, Sothern, Marie Tempest, Guitry, Gemier and the brothers Barrymore—all give testimony, in writing, painting, musicianship, poetry and dramatic authorship to æsthetic impulses other than acting. Since acting itself as an art is open to question, the merit or demerit of the performances produced from the æsthetic impulses in point is not an issue: the fact seems to be that it has been the artist who has become the actor rather than the actor who has become the artist.

The actor, as I have on another occasion hazarded, is the child of the miscegenation of an art and a trade: of the drama and the theatre. Since acting must appeal to the many—this is obviously its only reason for be-ing, for acting is primarily a filter through which drama may be lucidly distilled for heterogeneous theatre-goers—it must, logi-cally, be popular or perish. Surely no au-thentic art can rest or thrive upon such a pre-mise. The great actors and actresses, unlike great fashioners in other arts, have invariably been favourites of the crowd, and it is doubtless a too charitable hypothesis to assume that this crowd has ever been gifted with critical insight beyond cavil. If, therefore, the actor or actress who can sway great crowds is strictly to be termed an artist, why may we not also, by strict definition, similarly term as exponents of an authentic art others who can likewise sway the same crowds: a great politician like Roosevelt, say, or a great lecturer like Ingersoll, or a successful practical theologian like Billy Sunday? (Let us send out these paradox shock-troops to clear the way for the more sober infantry.)

I have said that I have no intention to argue for or against acting as an art yet, for all the circumstance that the case for the prosecution has long seemed the soundest and the most eloquent, there are still sporadic instances of imaginative histrionism that give one reason to ponder. But, pondering, it has subsequently come to the more penetrating critic that what has on such occasions passed for an art has in reality been merely a reflected art: the art of drama interpreted not with the imagination of the actor but, more precisely, *with the imagination of the dramatist*. In other words, that actor or actress is the most competent and effective whose imagination is successful in meeting literally, and translating, the imagination of the dramatist which has created the rôle played by the particular actor or actress. To name the actor's imagination in such a case a creative imagination is a rather wistful procedure, for it does not create but merely duplicates. Surely no advocate of acting as a creative art would be so bold as to contend that any actor, however great, has ever brought creative imagination to the already full and superb creative imagination of Shakespeare. This would be, on an actor's part, the sheerest impudence. The greatest actor is simply he who is best fitted by figure, voice, training and intelligence not to invade and annul the power of the rôle which a great dramatist has imagined and created. Duse and D'Annunzio were, so to speak, spiritually and physically one: hence the unmatched perfection of the former's histrionism in the latter's rôles. To see Duse is, save one admit one's self critically to the facts, therefore to suffer theoretical art doubts and the convictions of such as Mr. Daly.

It is, of course, the common habit of the prejudiced critic to overlook, in the estimate of acting as an art, the few admirable exponents of acting and to take into convenient consideration only the enormous majority of incompetents. But to argue that acting is not an art simply because a thousand Edmund Breeses and Miss Adele Bloods give no evidence that it is an art is to argue that sculpture is not an art simply because a thousand fashioners of Kewpies and plaster of Paris busts of Charlie Chaplin and Mr. Harding give no evidence in a like direction. Yet the circumstance that there are admittedly excellent actors as well as bad actors establishes acting as an art no more than the circumstance that there are admittedly excellent cuckoo-whistlers as well as bad cuckoo-whistlers es-

[89]

tablishes the playing of the cuckoo-whistle as an art. If I seem to reduce the comparison to what appears to be an absurdity, it is because by such absurdities, or elementals, is the status of acting in the field of the arts most sharply to be perceived. For if Bernhardt's ever-haunting cry of the heart in "Izeyl" is a peg, however slight, upon which may be hung a strand of the theory that maintains acting as an art, so too, by the strict canon of dialectics, is Mr. Ruben Katz's ever-haunting cry of the cuckoo in the coda of the slow movement of Beethoven's Pastoral Symphony.

If acting is an art, the proofs thus far offered are not only unconvincing but fundamentally, on the score of logic, not a little droll. Let us view a few illustrations. If criticism is an art (thus a familiar contention), why is not acting also an art, since both are concerned with re-creating works of art? But the artist's work offered up to the critic is a challenge, whereas the dramatist's work offered up to the actor is a consonance. Criticism is war, whether in behalf of æsthetic friend or against æsthetic foe; acting is agreement, peace. The critic re-creates, in terms of his own personality, the work of another and often emphatically different and antagonistic personality. The actor re-creates, in terms of a dramatist's concordantly imagined personality, his own personality: the result is less re-creation than non-re-creation. In other words, the less the actor creates or re-creates and the more he remains simply an adaptable tool in the hands of the dramatist, the better actor he is. The actor's state is thus what may be termed one of active impassivity. Originality and independence, save within the narrowest of limits, are denied him. He is a literal translator of a work of art, not an independently imaginative and speculative interpreter, as the critic is. The dramatist's work of art does not say to him, as to the critic, "Here I am! What do you, out of all your experience, taste and training, think of me?" It says to him, instead and peremptorily, "Here I am! Think of me exactly as I am, and adapt all of your experience, taste and training to the interpretation of me exactly as I am!"

Brushing aside the theory that the true artist is the actor who can transform his voice, his manner, his character; who will disappear behind his part instead of imposing himself on it and adding himself to it—a simple feat, since by such a definition the Messrs. Fregoli and Henri De Vries, amazing vaudeville protean actors, are true histrionic artists—Mr. Walkley, in his essay on "The English Actor of Today," bravely takes up the defence from what he regards as a more difficult approach. "In the art of acting as in any other art," he says, "the first requisite is life. The actor's part is a series of speeches and stage directions, mere cold print, an inert mass that has to be raised somehow from the dead. If the actor disappears behind it, there is nothing left but a Golgotha." Here is indeed gay news! Hamlet, Iago, Romeo, Shylock—mere "cold print," inert Shakespearian masses that, in order to live, have to be raised somehow from the dead by members of the Lambs' Club! It is only fair to add that Mr. Walkley quickly takes to cover after launching this torpedo, and devotes the balance of his interesting comments to a prudent and circumspect *pas seul* on the very middle of the controversial teeter-tawter. For no sooner has he described the majestic drama of Shakespeare as "mere cold print, an inert mass that has to be raised somehow from the dead," than he seems suddenly, and not without a touch of horror, to realize that he has ridiculously made of Shakespeare a mere blank canvas and pot of paint for the use of this or that actor whom he has named, by implication and with magnificent liberalness, a Raphael, or a mere slab of cold marble for the sculpturing skill of some socked and buskined Mercié.

II

Modern evaluation of acting as an unquestionable art takes its key from Rémond de Sainte-Albine, the girlishly ebullient Frenchman whose pragmatic critical credo was, "If it makes me feel, it is art." While it may be reasonable that a purely emotional art may aptly be criticized according to the degree of emotional reaction which it induces, it is the quality of emotion resident in the critic that offers that reasonableness a considerable confusion. A perfectly attuned and sound emotional equipment—an emotional equipment of absolute pitch, so to speak—is a rare thing, even among critics of brilliant intelligence, taste, imagination and experience. Goethe, Carlyle, Hazlitt, Dryden, Lessing, to mention only five, were physio-psychological units of dubious emotional structure, if we may trust the intimate chronicles. Thus, where much of their critical dramatic writing may be accepted without qualm, a distinct measure of distrust would attach itself to any critical estimate of acting which they might have written or actually did write.

There are, obviously, more or less definite standards whereby we may estimate critical writings of such men as these so far as those criticisms deal with what we may roughly describe as the cerebral or semi-cerebral arts, but there are no standards, even remotely determinable or exact, whereby we may appraise such of their criticisms as deal with the directly and wholly emotional art of acting. It is perhaps not too far a cry to assume that had Mr. William Archer's father been murdered shortly before Mr. Archer witnessed Mr. Forbes-Robertson's Hamlet, Mr. Archer would have been moved to believe Mr. Forbes-Robertson on even greater actor-artist than he believed him under the existing circumstances, or that had Mr. Otto Borchsenius, the Danish journalist-critic, regrettably found himself a victim of syphilis when he reviewed August Lindberg's "Oswald," he would have looked on the estimable Lindberg as a doubly impressive exponent of histrionism. Nothing is more æsthetically and artistically dubious and insecure than the appraisal of acting, for it is based upon the quicksands of varying human emotionalism, and of aural and visual prejudice. Were I, for example, one hundred times more proficient a critic of drama and life than I am, my criticism of acting would none the less remain often arbitrary and erratic, for I would remain constitutionally anæsthetic to a Juliet, however otherwise talented, who had piano legs, or to a Marc Antony who, for all his histrionic power, presented to the vision a pair of knock-knees. This, I well appreciate, is the kind of critical writing that is promptly set down as flippant, yet it is the truth so far as I am concerned and I daresay that it is, in one direction or another, the truth so far as the majority of critics are concerned.

The most that may be said of the soundness of this or that laudatory criticism of an actor's performance is that the performance in point has met exactly—or very nearly—the particular critic's personal notion of how he, as a human being, would have cried, laughed and otherwise comported himself were he an actor and were he in the actor's rôle. The opposite, or denunciatory, phase of such criticism holds a similar truth. If this is not true, by what standards *can* the critic estimate the actor's performance? By the standards of the actors who have preceded this actor in the playing of the rôle, you say? What if the rôle is a new one, a peculiar and novel one, that has not been played before? Again, you say that

the rôle may be in an alien drama and that
the actor may be an alien, both rôle and
performance being foreign to the emotional
equipment of the critic. But basic emotions, the foundation of drama, are universal.
Still again, what of such dramas as "Œdipus
Rex," what of such rôles—this with a triumphant chuckle on your part? I return the
chuckle, and bid you read the criticisms that
have been written of the actors who have
played in these rôles! Invariably the actors
have been treated in precisely the same terms
and by the same standards as if they were
playing, not in the drama of the fifth century
before Christ, but in "Fedora," "The Face in
the Moonlight" or "The Count of Monte
Cristo."

One cannot imagine sound criticism apply-
ing to any authentic art the standard of actor
criticism that I have noted. Criticism, true
enough, is always more or less personal, but,
in its operation upon the authentic arts, its
personality is ever like a new bottle into which
the vintage wine of art has been poured.

Criticism of the authentic arts is the result of the impact of a particular art upon a particular critical personality. Criticism of the dubious art of acting is the result of the impact of a particular critical personality upon this or that instance of acting. But if this is even remotely true, you inquire ironically, what of such an excellent instance of acting as Mimi Aguglia's "Salome"; how in God's name may the critic appraise that performance in the manner set down, i. e., in terms of himself were he a stage performer? Well, for all the surface humours of the question, that is actually more or less the way in which he does appraise it. The actor or actress, unlike the artist in more authentic fields, may never interpret emotion in a manner unfamilar to the critic: the interpretation must be a reflection, more or less stereotyped, of the critic's repertoire of emotions. Thus, where art is original expression, acting is merely the audible expression of a silent expression. In another phrase, expression in acting is predicated upon, and limited by, the expression of the critic. It is, therefore, a mere duplication of expression. And what holds true in the case of the critic so far as acting is concerned obviously holds doubly true in the case of the uncritical public.

Re-reading the celebrated critiques of acting, I come to the conclusion that the word "art" has almost uniformly been applied to acting by critics who, thinking that they had perhaps belaboured the subject a trifle too severely, were disposed graciously to throw it a sop. As good an illustration as any may be had from Lewes, certainly a friend of acting if ever there was one. Thus Lewes:

"The truth is, we exaggerate the talent of an actor because we judge only from the effect he produces, without inquiring too curiously into the means. But, while the painter has nothing but his canvas and the author has nothing but white paper and printers' ink with which to produce his effects, the actor has all other arts as handmaids; the poet labours for him, creates his part, gives him his eloquence, his music, his imagery, his tenderness, his pathos, his sublimity; the scene-painter aids him; the costumes, the lights, the music, all the

[99]

fascination of the stage—all subserve the actor's effects; these raise him upon a pedestal; remove them, and what is he? He who can make a stage mob bend and sway with his eloquence, what could he do with a real mob, no poet by to prompt him? He who can charm us with the stateliest imagery of a noble mind, when robed in the sables of Hamlet, or in the toga of Coriolanus, what can he do in coat and trousers on the world's stage? Rub off the paint, and the eyes are no longer brilliant! Reduce the actor to his intrinsic value, and then weigh him with the rivals whom he surpasses in reputation and fortune. . . . If my estimate of the intrinsic value of acting is lower than seems generally current, it is from no desire to disparage *an art* I have always loved; but, etc., etc."

You will find the same dido in most of the essays on acting: a protracted series of cuffs and slaps terminating in a gentle non-sequitur kiss.

Acting at its finest is, however, often a confusing hypnosis; it is not to be wondered at that, fresh from its spell, the critic has mistaken it for a more exalted something than it intrinsically is. The flame and fire of a Duse, the haunt and magic of a Bernhardt, the powerful stage sense of creation of a Moissi—these are not a little befuddling. And, under their serpent-like charm, it is not incomprehensible that the critic should confound effect and cause. Yet acting, even of the highest order, is intrinsically akin to the legerdemain of a Hermann or a Kellar with a Shakespeare or a Molière as an assistant to hand over, as the moment bids, the necessary pack of cards or bowl of goldfish. It is trickery raised to its most exalted level: a combination of experience, intelligence and great charm, not revivifying something cold and dead, but releasing something quick and alive from the prison of the printed page.

The actor who contends in favour of his creative art that he must experience within him the feeling of the dramatist, that he must actually persuade himself to feel his rôle with all its turning smiles and tears, speaks nonsense. So, too, must the auditor, yet who would term the auditor a creative artist? The actor who contends in favour of his creative

art the exact opposite, that he is, to wit, a
creative artist since he must theatrically create
the dramatist's moods, illusions and emotions
without feeling them himself, also speaks nonsense. For so, too, in such a case as "Electra," or "Ghosts," or "No More Blondes,"
must the auditor, yet who, again, would term
the latter a creative artist? The actor who
contends in favour of his creative art that two
accomplished actors often "create" the same
rôle in an entirely different manner, speaks
nonsense yet again. For what is not creation
in the first place does not become creation
merely because it is multiplied by two. The
actor who further contends in behalf of his
creative art that if effective acting were the
mere trickery that some maintain it to be, any
person ordinarily gifted should be able, after
a little experiment, to give an effective stage
performance, speaks truer than he knows.
Some of the most remarkable performances
on the stage of the Abbey Theatre of Dublin
have been given by just such persons. And

there are numerous other instances. If acting is an art—and I do not say that it may not be—it at least, as an art, ill bears cross-examination of even the most superficial nature.

III

Acting is perhaps less an art than the deceptive echo of an art. It is drama's exalted halloo come back to drama from the walls of the surrounding amphitheatre. Criticism of acting too often mistakes the echo for the original voice. Although the analogy wears motley, criticism of this kind operates in much the same manner as if it were to contend that an approximately exact and beautiful Ben Ali Haggin *tableau vivant* reproduction of, say, Velasquez's "The Spinners," was creative art in the sense that the original is creative art. Acting is to the art of the drama much what these so-called living pictures are to the art of painting. If acting is to be termed an art, it is, like the living picture, a freak art, an art with belladonna in its eyes and ever, even at its highest, a bit grotesque.

In his defence of acting as an art equal to that of poetry and literature, Henry Irving has observed, "It has been said that acting is unworthy because it represents feigned emotions, but this censure would apply with equal force to poet or novelist." But would it? The poet and the novelist may feign emotions, but it is their own active imaginations which feign them. The actor merely feigns passively the emotions which the imagination of the poet has actively feigned; if there is feigning, the actor merely parrots it. If there is feigned emotion in, say, the second stanza of Swinburne's "Rococo," and I mount an illuminated platform and recite the stanza very eloquently and impressively, am I precisely feigning the emotion of it or am I merely feigning the emotion that the great imagination of Swinburne has feigned? Feigned or unfeigned, the emotions of the poet come ready-made to the heart and lips of the actor.

[104]

The Place of Acting

Continues Irving further: "It is the actor who gives body to the ideas of the highest dramatic literature—fire, force, and sensibility, without which they would remain for most people mere airy abstractions." What one engages here is the peculiar logic that acting is an art since it popularizes dramatic literature and makes it intelligible to a majority of dunderheads!

One more quotation from this actor's defence, and we may pass on. "The actor's work is absolutely concrete," he challenges. "He is brought in every phase of his work into direct comparison with existing things. . . . Not only must his dress be suitable to the part which he assumes, but his bearing must not be in any way antagonistic to the spirit of the time in which the play is fixed. The free bearing of the sixteenth century is distinct from the artificial one of the seventeenth, the mannered one of the eighteenth, and the careless one of the nineteenth. . . . The voice must be modulated to the vogue of the time. The habitual action of a rapier-bearing age is different from that of a mail-clad one—nay, the armour of a period ruled in real life the poise and bearing of the body; and all this must be reproduced on the stage. . . . *It cannot therefore be seriously put forward in the face of such manifold requirements that no Art is required for the representation of suitable action!"* The italics are those of one who experiences some difficulty in persuading himself that if Art is required for such things as these—dress, carriage, modulation of voice and carrying a sword—Art, strictly speaking, is no less required in the matter of going to a Quat'-z-Arts costume ball.

Acting is perhaps best to be criticized not as art but as colourful and impressive artifice. Miss Margaret Anglin's Joan of Arc is a more or less admirable example of acting not because it is art but because it is a shrewd, vivid and beguiling synthesis of various intrinsically spurious dodges: black tights to make stout Anglo-Saxon limbs appear Gallicly slender, a telescoping of words containing the sound of *s* to conceal a personal defect in the structure of the upper lip, a manœuvring of the central action up stage to emphasize, through a familiar trick of the theatre, the sympathetic frailty of the character which the actress herself physically lacks, two intakes of breath before a shout of defiance that the effect of the ring of the directly antecedent shout on the part of one of the inquisitors may be diminished. . . . An effective acting performance is like a great explosion; and as T N T is made from nitric acid, which is in turn made from such nitrates as potassium nitrate or saltpeter, which are in turn derived from the salts of decomposed guano, so is a great explosion of histrionism similarly made and derived from numerous—and not infrequently ludicrous and even vulgar—basic elements.

The ill-balanced species of criticism which appraises an histrionic performance as art on the sole ground of the hypnotic effect it produces, with no inquiry into the means whereby that effect is produced, might analogously, were it to pursue this logic, appraise similarly as art the performance of an adept literal hypnotist. And with logic perhaps much more sound. For if acting as an art is to be appraised in the degree of the effect it imparts to, and induces in, the auditor-spectator, surely—if there is any sense at all in such a method of estimate—may certain other such performances as I have suggested be similarly appraised. Criticism rests upon a foundation of logic; whatever it may deal with—æsthetics, emotions, what not—it cannot remove itself entirely from that foundation. Thus, if Mr. John Barrymore is an artist because, by identifying the heart and mind of his auditor-spectator with some such character as Fedya and by suggesting directly that character's tragic dégringolade, he can make the auditor-spectator pity and cry, so too an artist—by the rigid canon of æsthetic criticism—was Friedrich Anton Mesmer, who is said to have been able to do the same thing.

What I attempt here is no facile paradox, but a *reductio ad absurdum* designed to show up the fallacy of the prevailing method of

[108]

actor criticism. In criticism of the established arts, there is no such antic deportment. The critic never confuses the stimulations of jazz music with those of sound music, nor the stimulations of open melodrama with those of more profound drama. From each of these he receives stimulations of a kind: some superficial, some deep. But he inquires, in each instance, into the means whereby the various stimulations were vouchsafed to him. While he recognizes the fact that the sudden and unexpected shooting off of a revolver in "Secret Service" produces in him a sensation of shock as great as the sudden and unexpected shooting off of a revolver in "Hedda Gabler," he does not therefore promptly, and with no further reasoning, conclude that the two sensations are of an æsthetic piece. Nor does he assume that, since the nervous effect of the fall to death in "The Green Goddess" and of the fall to death in "The Master Builder" affect him immediately in much the same way, both sensations are accordingly produced by sound artistic means. Nor, yet again, does he confuse the quality—nor the springs of that quality—of the mood of wistful pathos with which "Poor Butterfly" and "Porgi, Amor" inspire him. But this confusion persists as part and parcel of the bulk of the criticism of acting. For one Hazlitt, or Lamb, or Lewes, or Anatole France who retains, or has retained, his clear discernment before the acted drama, there are, and have been, a number tenfold who have confounded the wonders of the phonograph with the wonders of Josef Haydn.

V. DRAMATIC CRITICISM

V. DRAMATIC CRITICISM

I

ARTHUR BINGHAM WALKLEY begins one of the best books ever written on the subject thus: "It is not to be gainsaid that the word criticism has gradually acquired a certain connotation of contempt. . . . Every one who expresses opinions, however imbecile, in print calls himself a 'critic.' The greater the ignoramus, the greater the likelihood of his posing as a 'critic.' " An excellent book, as I have said, with a wealth of sharp talk in it, but Mr. Walkley seems to me to err somewhat in his preliminary assumption. Criticism has acquired a connotation of contempt less because it is practised by a majority of ignoramuses than because it is accepted at full face value by an infinitely greater majority of ignoramuses. It is not the mob that curls a lip—the mob accepts the lesser ignoramus at his own estimate of himself; it is the lonely and negligible minority man who, pausing musefully in the field that is the world, contemplates the jackasses eating the daisies.

No man is so contemptuous of criticism as the well-stocked critic, just as there is no man so contemptuous of clothes as the man with the well-stocked wardrobe. It is as impossible to imagine a critic like Shaw not chuckling derisively at criticism as it is to imagine a regular subscriber to the *Weekly Review* not swallowing it whole. The experienced critic, being on the inside, is in a position to look into the heads of the less experienced, and to see the wheels go round. He is privy to all their monkeyshines, since he is privy to his own. Having graduated from quackery, he now smilingly regards others still at the trade of seriously advancing sure cures for æsthetic baldness, cancer, acne and trifacial neuralgia. And while the yokels rub in the lotions and swallow the pills, he permits himself a small, but eminently sardonic, hiccup.

It is commonly believed that the first virtue

of a critic is honesty. As a matter of fact, in four cases out of five, honesty is the last virtue of a critic. As criticism is practised in America, honesty presents itself as the leading fault. There is altogether too much honesty. The greater the blockhead, the more honest he is. And as a consequence the criticism of these blockheads, founded upon their honest convictions, is worthless. There is some hope for an imbecile if he is dishonest, but none if he is resolute in sticking to his idiocies. If the average American critic were to cease writing what he honestly believes and dishonestly set down what he doesn't believe, the bulk of the native criticism would gain some common sense and take on much of the sound value that it presently lacks. Honesty is a toy for first-rate men; when lesser men seek to play with it and lick off the paint, they come down with colic.

It is further maintained that enthusiasm is a supplementary desideratum in a critic, that unless he is possessed of enthusiasm he cannot impart a warm love for fine things to his

reader. Surely this, too, is nonsense. Enthusiasm is a virtue not in the critic, but in
the critic's reader. And such desired enthusiasm can be directly generated by enthusiasm
no more than a glyceryl nitrate explosion can
be generated by sulfuric acid. Enthusiasm
may be made so contagious as to elect a man
president of the United States or to raise an
army large enough to win a world war, but
it has never yet been made sufficiently contagious to persuade one American out of a hundred thousand that Michelangelo's David of
the Signoria is a better piece of work than the
Barnard statue of Lincoln. Enthusiasm is
an attribute of the uncritical, the defectively
educated: stump speakers, clergymen, young
girls, opera-goers, Socialists, Italians, such
like. And not only an attribute, but a
weapon. But the cultivated and experienced
man has as little use for enthusiasm as for indignation. He appreciates that while it may
convert a pack of ignoble doodles, it can't convert any one worth converting. The latter
must be persuaded, not inflamed. He real-

izes that where a double brass band playing "Columbia, the Gem of the Ocean" may leave a civilized Englishman cold to the virtues of the United States, proof that the United States has the best bathroom plumbing in the world may warm him up a bit. The sound critic is not a cheer leader, but a referee. Art is hot, criticism cold. Aristotle's criticism of Euripides is as placid and reserved as Mr. William Archer's criticism of the latest drama at the St. James's Theatre; Brunetière is as calm over his likes as Mr. H. T. Parker of the Boston *Transcript*. There is no more enthusiasm in Lessing than there is indignation in Walkley. Hazlitt, at a hundred degrees emotional Fahrenheit, remains critically cool as a cucumber. To find enthusiasm, you will have to read the New York *Times*.

Enthusiasm, in short, is the endowment of immaturity. The greater the critic, the greater his disinclination to communicate æsthetic heat. Such communication savours of propaganda and, however worthy that

[117]

propaganda, he will have naught to do with its trafficking. If the ability to possess and communicate enthusiasm is the mark of the true critic, then the theatrical page of the New York *Journal* is the greatest critical literature in America.

A third contention has it that aloofness and detachment are no less valuable to the dramatic critic than honesty and enthusiasm. Unless I am seriously mistaken, also bosh. Dramatic criticism is fundamentally the critic's art of appraising himself in terms of various forms of drama. Or, as I some time ago put it, the only sound dramatic critic is the one who reports less the impression that this or that play makes upon him than the impression he makes upon this or that play. Of all the forms of criticism, dramatic criticism is essentially, and perhaps correctly, the most personal. Tell me what a dramatic critic eats and drinks, how far north of Ninetieth Street he lives, what he considers a pleasant evening when he is not in the theatre, and what kind of lingerie his wife wears, and I'll tell you

[118]

with very few misses what kind of critic he is.
I'll tell you whether he is fit to appreciate
Schnitzler, or whether he is fit only for Augustus Thomas. I'll tell you in advance what
he will think about, and how he will react to,
Hauptmann, Sacha Guitry or George V.
Hobart. I'll tell you whether he is the sort
that makes a great to-do when his eagle eye
spots Sir Nigel Waterhouse, M. P., in Act II
fingering a copy of the Philadelphia *Public
Ledger* instead of the London *Times,* and
whether he is the sort that writes "Mr. John
Cort has staged the play in his customary
lavish manner" when the rise of the curtain
discloses to him a room elaborately decorated
in the latest Macy mode. To talk about the
value of detachment in a dramatic critic is to
talk about the value of detachment in a
Swiss mountain guide. The criticism is the
man; the man the criticism.

Of all forms of criticism, dramatic criticism is the most purely biological. Were the
genii to put the mind of Max Beerbohm into
the head of Mr. J. Ranken Towse, and vice

versa, their criticisms would still remain exactly as they are. But, on the contrary, were the head of Mr. J. Ranken Towse to be placed on the body of Max Beerbohm, and vice versa, their criticisms would take on points of view diametrically opposed to their present. Max would begin admiring the Rev. Dr. Charles Rann Kennedy and Towse would promptly proceed to put on his glasses to get a better view of the girl on the end. Every book of dramatic criticism—every single piece of dramatic criticism—is a searching, illuminating autobiography. The dramatic critic performs a clinic upon himself every time he takes his pen in his hand. He may try, as Walkley puts it, to substitute for the capital I's "nouns of multitude signifying many," or some of those well-worn stereotypes—"It is thought," "one may be pardoned for hinting," "will any one deny?" etc., etc.—by which criticism keeps up the pretence that it is not a man but a corporation, but he fools no one.

To ask the dramatic critic to keep himself out of his criticism, to detach himself, is thus

[120]

a trifle like asking an actor to keep himself out
of his rôle. Dramatic critics and actors are
much alike. The only essential difference is
that the actor does his acting on a platform.
But, platform or no platform, the actor and
the dramatic critic best serve their rôles when
they filter them through their own personalities. A dramatic critic who is told to keep
his personality out of his criticism is in the
position of an actor who, being physically and
temperamentally like Mr. John Barrymore, is
peremptorily directed by a producer to stick
a sofa pillow under his belt, put on six extra
heel-lifts, acquire a whiskey voice and play
Falstaff like the late Sir Herbert Tree. The
best dramatic critics from the time of Quintus
Horatius Flaccus (*vide* the "Epistola") have
sunk their vivid personalities into their work
right up to the knees. Not only have they described the adventures of their souls among
masterpieces, but the adventures of their kid-
neys, spleens and *cæca* as well. Each has held
the mirror of drama up to his own nature,
with all its idiosyncrasies. And in it have

been sharply reflected not the cut and dried features of the professor, but the vital features of a red-alive man. The other critics have merely held up the mirror to these red-alive men, and have reflected not themselves but the latter. Then, in their vainglory, they have looked again into the handglass and have mistaken the reflection of the parrot for an eagle.

A third rubber-stamp: the critic must have sympathy. As properly contend that a surgeon must have sympathy. The word is misused. What the critic must have is not sympathy, which in its common usage bespeaks a measure of sentimental concern, but interest. If a dramatic critic, for example, has sympathy for an actress he can no more criticize her with poise than a surgeon can operate on his own wife. The critic may on occasion have sympathy as the judge in a court of law may on occasion have it, but if he is a fair critic, or a fair judge, he can't do anything about it, however much he would like to. Between the fair defendant in the lace baby collar and a soft heart, Article X, Section 123, Page 416, absurdly interposes itself. (In example, being a human being with a human being's weaknesses before a critic, I would often rather praise a lovely one when she is bad than an unlovely one when she is good—and, alas, I fear that I sometimes do—but in the general run I try to remember my business and behave myself. It isn't always easy. But I do my best, and angels and Lewes could do no more.) The word sympathy is further mishandled, as in the similar case of the word enthusiasm. What a critic should have is not, as is common, sympathy and enthusiasm *before* the fact, but *after* it. The critic who enters a theatre bubblingly certain that he is going to have a good time is no critic. The critic is he who leaves a theatre cheerfully certain that he *has* had a good time. Sympathy and enthusiasm, unless they are *ex post facto,* are precisely like prevenient prejudice and hostility. Sympathy has no more preliminary place in the equipment of a critic than in the equipment of an ambulance driver or a

[123]

manufacturer of bird cages. It is the caboose
of criticism, not the engine.

The trouble with dramatic criticism in
America, speaking generally, is that where it
is not frankly reportorial it too often seeks to
exhibit a personality when there exists no personality to exhibit. Himself perhaps conscious of this lack, the critic indulges in heroic
makeshifts to inject into his writings a note of
individuality, and the only individuality that
comes out of his perspirations is of a piece
with that of the bearded lady or the dog-
faced boy. Individuality of this freak species
is the bane of the native criticism. The college professor who, having nothing to say, tries
to give his criticism an august air by figura-
tively attaching to it a pair of whiskers and
horn glasses, the suburban college professor
who sedulously practises an aloofness from the
madding crowd that his soul longs to be part
of, the college professor who postures as a
man of the world, the newspaper reporter who
postures as a college professor, the journalist
who performs in terms of Art between the

Saks and Gimbel advertisements—these and others like them are the sad comedians in the tragical crew. In their heavy attempts to live up to their fancy dress costumes, in their laborious efforts to conceal their humdrum personalities in the uncomfortable gauds of Petruchio and Gobbo, they betray themselves even to the bus boys. The same performer cannot occupy the rôles of Polonius and Hamlet, even in a tank town troupe.

No less damaging to American dramatic criticism is the dominant notion that criticism, to be valuable, must be constructive. That is, that it must, as the phrase has it, "build up" rather than "tear down." As a result of this conviction we have an endless repertoire of architectonic advice from critics wholly without the structural faculty, advice which, were it followed, would produce a drama twice as poor as that which they criticize. Obsessed with the idea that they must be constructive, the critics know no lengths to which they will not go in their sweat to dredge up cures of one sort or another. They constructively point out that Shaw's plays would be better plays if Shaw understood the punctual technique of Pinero, thus destroying a "Cæsar and Cleopatra" to construct a "Second Mrs. Tanqueray." They constructively point out the trashy aspect of some Samuel Shipman's "Friendly Enemies," suggest more serious enterprises to him, and get the poor soul to write a "The Unwritten Chapter" which is ten times as bad. They are not content to be critics; they must also be playwrights. They stand in mortal fear of the old recrimination, "He who can, does; he who can't, criticizes," not pausing to realize that the names of Mr. Octavus Roy Cohen and Matthew Arnold may be taken as somewhat confounding respective examples. They note with some irritation that the critic for the Wentzville, Mo., *Beacon* is a destructive critic, but are conveniently ignorant of the fact—which may conceivably prove something more—that so was George Farquhar. If destructive criticism, in their meaning, is criticism which pulls down without building up in return, three-fourths of the best dramatic criticism written since the time of Boileau, fully filling the definition, is worthless. One can't cure a yellow fever patient by pointing out to him that he should have caught the measles. One can't improve the sanitary condition of a neighbourhood merely by giving the outhouse a different coat of paint. The foe of destructive criticism is the pro-German of American art.

Our native criticism suffers further from the commercial Puritanism of its mediums. What is often mistaken for the Puritanism of the critic is actually the commercial Puritanism forced upon him by the owner and publisher of the journal in which his writings appear, and upon which he has to depend for a livelihood. Although this owner and publisher is often not personally the Puritan, he is yet shrewdly aware that the readers of his journal are, and out of this awareness he becomes what may be termed a circulation bluenose. Since circulation and advertising revenue are twins, he must see to it that the sensibilities of the former are not offended. And his circumspection, conveyed to the critic by the copy reader or perhaps only sensed, brings about the Puritan play-acting by the critic. This accounts to no little degree for the hostile and uncritical reviews of even the most finished risqué farces, and of the best efforts of American and European playwrights to depict truthfully and fairly the more unpleasant phases of sex. "I agree with you that this last naughty farce of Avery Hopwood's is awfully funny stuff," a New York newspaper reviewer once said to me; "I laughed at it until my ribs ached; but I don't dare write as much. One can't praise such things in a paper with the kind of circulation that ours has." It is criticism bred from this commercial Puritanism that has held back farce writing in America, and I venture to say much serious dramatic writing as well. The best farce of a Guitry or a Dieudonné, produced in America today without childish excisions, would receive unfavourable notices from nine newspapers out of ten. The best sex drama of a Porto-Riche or a Wedekind

would suffer—indeed, already has suffered—
a similar fate. I predicted to Eugene
O'Neill, the moment I laid down the manuscript of his pathological play "Diff'rent," the
exact manner in which, two months later, the
axes fell upon him.

For one critic like Mr. J. Ranken Towse
who is a Puritan by tradition and training,
there are a dozen who are Puritans by proxy.
One can no more imagine a dramatic critic on
a newspaper owned by Mr. Cyrus H. K. Cur-
tis praising Schnitzler's "Reigen" or Rip's and
Gignoux's "Scandale de Deauville" than one
can imagine the same critic denouncing "Ben
Hur." What thus holds true in journalistic
criticism holds true in precisely the same way
in the criticism written by the majority of
college professors. I doubt that there is a
college professor in America today who, however much he admired a gay, reprobate farce
like "Le Rubicon" or "L'Illusioniste," would
dare state his admiration in print. Puritan
or no Puritan, it is professionally necessary
for him to comport himself as one. His uni-

versity demands it, silently, sternly, idiotically. He is the helpless victim of its æsthetic Ku Klux. Behind any drama dealing unconventionally with sex, there hovers a spectre that vaguely resembles Professor Scott Nearing. He sees it . . . he reflects . . . he works up a safe indignation.

Dramatic criticism travels, in America, carefully laid tracks. Signal lights, semaphores and one-legged old men with red flags are stationed along the way to protect it at the crossings, to make it safe, and to guard it from danger. It elaborately steams, pulls, puffs, chugs, toots, whistles, grinds and rumbles for three hundred miles—and brings up at something like Hinkletown, Pa. It is eager, but futile. It is honest, but so is Dr. Frank Crane. It is fearless, but so is the actor who plays the hero strapped to the papier-mâché buzz-saw. It is constructive, but so is an embalmer. It is detached, but so is a man in the Fiji Islands. It is sympathetic, but so is a quack prostatitician.

VI. DRAMATIC CRITICISM IN AMERICA

VI. DRAMATIC CRITICISM IN AMERICA

I

DRAMATIC criticism, at its best, is the adventure of an intelligence among emotions. The chief end of drama is the enkindling of emotions; the chief end of dramatic criticism is to rush into the burning building and rescue the metaphysical weaklings who are wont to be overcome by the first faint whiffs of smoke.

Dramatic criticism, in its common run, fails by virtue of its confusion of unschooled emotion with experienced emotion. A dramatic critic who has never been kissed may properly appreciate the readily assimilable glories of "Romeo and Juliet," but it is doubtful that he will be able properly to appreciate the somewhat more evasive splendours of "Liebelei." The capability of a judge does

not, of course, depend upon his having himself once been in jail, nor does the capability
of a critic depend upon his having personally
once experienced the emotions of the dramatis personæ, but that critic is nevertheless the
most competent whose emotions the dramatis
personæ do not so much anticipatorily stir up
as recollectively soothe.

All criticism is more or less a statement in
terms of the present of what one has viewed
of the past through a delicate, modern reduc-
ing-glass. Intelligence is made up, in large
part, of dead emotions; ignorance, of emotions that have lived on, deaf and dumb and
crippled, but ever smiling. The general ad-
mission that a dramatic critic must be experienced in drama, literature, acting and theories
of production but not necessarily in emotions
is somewhat difficult of digestion. Such a
critic may conceivably comprehend much of
Sheridan, Molière, Bernhardt and Yevrey-
noff, but a hundred searching and admirable
things like the beginning of "Anatol," the
middle of "Lonely Lives" and the end of

"The Case of Rebellious Susan" must inevitably be without his ken, and baffle his efforts at sound penetration. I do not here posture myself as one magnificently privy to all the mysteries, but rather as one who, failing perhaps to be on very intimate terms with them, detects and laments the deficiencies that confound him. Experience, goeth the saw, is a wise master. But it is, for the critic, an even wiser slave. A critic on the Marseilles *Petits Pois* may critically admire "La Dernière Nuit de Don Juan," but it takes an Anatole France critically to understand it.

The superficial quality of American emotions, sociological and æsthetic, enjoyed by the great majority of American critics, operates extensively against profundity in American criticism—in that of literature and music no less than that of drama. American emotions, speaking in the mass, where they are not the fixed and obvious emotions ingenerate in most countries—such as love of home, family and country, and so on—are one-syllable emotions, primary-colour emotions. The polysyllabic and pastel emotions are looked on as dubious, even degenerate. No man, for example, who, though absolutely faithful to his wife, confessed openly that he had winked an eye at a ballet girl could conceivably be elected to membership in the Union League Club. The man who, after a cocktail, indiscreetly gave away the news that he had felt a tear of joy in his eye when he heard the minuet of Mozart's G minor symphony or a tear of sadness when he looked upon Corot's "La Solitude," would be promptly set down by the other members of the golf club as a dipsomaniac who was doubtless taking narcotics on the side. If a member of the Y. M. C. A. were to glance out of the window and suddenly ejaculate, "My, what a beautiful girl!" the superintendent would immediately grab him by the seat of the pantaloons and throw him down the back stairs. And if a member of the American Legion were to sniffle so much as once when the orchestra in the Luna Park dance hall played "Wiener Blut," a spy would seize him by the ear and hurry him be-

[136]

fore the heads of the organization as a suspicious fellow, in all probability of German blood.

The American is either ashamed of honest emotion or, if he is not ashamed, is soon shamed into shame by his neighbours. He is profoundly affected by any allusion to Mother, the Baby, or the Flag—the invincible trinity of American dramatic hokum—and his reactions thereto meet with the full favour of church and state; but he is unmoved, he is silently forbidden to be moved, by a love that doesn't happen to fall into the proper pigeonhole, by a work of great beauty that doesn't happen to preach a backwoods Methodist sermon, by sheer loveliness, or majesty, or unadorned truth. And this corsetted emotion, mincing, wasp-waisted and furtive, colours all native criticism. It makes the dramatic critic ashamed of simple beauty, and forbids him honestly to admire the mere loveliness of such exhibitions as Ziegfeld's. It makes him ashamed of passion, and forbids him honestly to admire such excellent dramas as Georges de

Porto-Riche's "Amoureuse." It makes him ashamed of laughter, and forbids him to chuckle at the little naughtinesses of Sacha Guitry and his own Avery Hopwood. It makes him ashamed of truth, and forbids him to regard with approbation such a play as "The Only Law." The American drama must therefore not create new emotions for him, but must hold the battered old mirror up to his own. It must warm him not with new, splendid and worldly emotions, but must satisfy him afresh as to the integrity and higher merit of his own restricted parcel of emotions. It must abandon all new, free concepts of love and life, of romance and adventure and glory, and must reassure him—with appropriate quiver-music—that the road to heaven is up Main Street and the road to hell down the Avenue de l'Opéra.

Though there is a regrettable trace of snobbery in the statement, it yet remains that—with half a dozen or so quickly recognizable exceptions—the practitioners of dramatic criticism in America are in the main a humbly-

born, underpaid and dowdy-lived lot. This
was as true of them yesterday as it is today.
And as Harlem, delicatessen-store dinners,
napkin-rings and the Subway are not, perhaps, best conducive to a polished and suavely
cosmopolitan outlook on life and romance and
enthralling beauty, we have had a dramatic
criticism pervaded by a vainglorious homeli-
ness, by a side-street æsthetic, and by not a
little of the difficultly suppressed rancour that
human nature ever feels in the presence of admired yet unachievable situations. Up to
fifteen years ago, drama in America was com-
pelled critically to meet with, and adhere
strictly to, the standards of life, culture and
romance as they obtained over on Mr. William Winter's Staten Island. Since Winter's
death, it has been urged critically to abandon
the standards of Staten Island and comply
instead with the eminently more sophisticated
standards derived from a four years' study of
Cicero, Stumpf and the Norwegian system of
communal elections at Harvard or Catawba
College, combined with a two weeks' stay in

Paris. For twenty years, Ibsen and Pinero suffered the American critical scourge because they had not been born and brought up in a town with a bust of Cotton Mather or William Cullen Bryant in its public square, and did not think quite the same way about things as Horace Greeley. For twenty years more, Porto-Riche and Frenchmen like him will doubtless suffer similarly because, in a given situation, they do not act precisely as Mr. Frank A. Munsey or Dr. Stuart Pratt Sherman would; for twenty years more, Hauptmann and other Germans will doubtless be viewed with a certain measure of condescension because they have not enjoyed the same advantages as Professor Brander Matthews in buying Liberty Bonds, at par.

American dramatic criticism is, and always has been, essentially provincial. It began by mistaking any cheap melodrama like "The Charity Ball" or "The Wife" which was camouflaged with a few pots of palms and half a dozen dress suits for a study of American society. It progressed by appraising as the

dean of American dramatists and as the leading American dramatic thinker a playwright
who wrote such stuff as "All over this great
land thousands of trains run every day, start-
ing and arriving in punctual agreement because this is a woman's world! The great
steamships, dependable almost as the sun—a
million factories in civilization—the countless
looms and lathes of industry—the legions of
labour that weave the riches of the world—all
—all move by the mainspring of man's faith
in woman!" It has come to flower today in
denouncing what the best European critics
have proclaimed to be the finest example of
American fantastic comedy on the profound
ground that "it is alien to American mor-
ality," and in hailing as one of the most acute
studies of a certain typical phase of American
life a comedy filched substantially from the
French.

The plush-covered provincialism of the native dramatic criticism, operating in this wise
against conscientious drama and sound appreciation of conscientious drama, constantly

betrays itself for all the chintz hocus-pocus
with which it seeks drolly to conceal that provincialism. For all its easy incorporation of
French phrases laboriously culled from the
back of Webster, its casually injected allu-
sions to the Überbrett'l, Stanislav Pshibui-
shevsky, the excellent *cuissot de Chevreuil
sauce poivrade* to be had in the little restaurant
near the comfort station in the Place Pigalle,
and the bewitching eyes of the prima ballerina
in the 1917 Y. M. C. A. show at Epernay, it
lets its mask fall whenever it is confronted in
the realistic flesh by one or another of the very
things against which it has postured its cosmopolitanism. Thus does the mask fall, and
reveal the old pair of suburban eyes, before
the "indelicacy" of French dramatic masterpieces, before the "polished wit" of British
polished witlessness, before the "stodginess"
of the German master depictions of stodgy
German peasantry, before the "gloom" of
Russian dramatic photography, before the
"sordidness" of "Countess Julie" and the
"wholesomeness" of "The Old Homestead."

Cosmopolitanism is a heritage, not an acqui-
sition.   It may be born to a man in a wooden
shack in Hardin County, in Kentucky, or in
a little cottage in Hampshire in England, or
in a garret of Paris, but, unless it is so born
to him, a thousand Cunard liners and Orient
Expresses cannot bring it to him.   All criticism is geography of the mind and geometry
of the heart.   American criticism suffers in
that what æsthetic wanderlust its mind experiences is confined to excursion trips, and in
that what x its heart seeks to discover is an
unknown quantity only to emotional sub-
freshmen.

Criticism is personal, or it is nothing.   Talk
to me of impersonal criticism, and I'll talk to
you of impersonal sitz-bathing.   Impersonal
criticism is the dodge of the critic without personality.   Some men marry their brother's
widow; some earn a livelihood imitating
George M. Cohan; some write impersonal
criticism.   Show me how I can soundly criticize Mrs. Fiske as Hannele without comment-
ing on the mature aspect of the lady's *stentop-*

gia, and I shall begin to believe that there may
be something in the impersonal theory. Show
me how I can soundly criticize the drama of
Wedekind without analyzing Wedekind, the
man, and I shall believe in the theory to the
full. It is maintained by the apostles of the
theory that the dramatic critic is in the position of a judge in the court of law: that his
concern, like that of the latter, is merely with
the evidence presented to him, not with the
personalities of those who submit the evidence.
Nothing could be more idiotic. The judge
who does not take into consideration, for example, that—whatever the nature of the evidence—the average Italian, or negro, or Ar-
menian before him is in all probability lying
like the devil is no more equipped to be a
sound judge than the dramatic critic who, for
all the stage evidence, fails to take into consideration that Strindberg personally was a
lunatic, that Pinero, while treating of British
impulses and character, is himself of ineradicable Portuguese mind and blood, that the inspiration of D'Annunzio came not from a

[144]

woman out of life but from a woman out of the greenroom, and that Shaw is a legal virgin.

Just as dramatic criticism, as it is practised in America, is Mason-jar criticism—criticism, that is, obsessed by a fixed determination to put each thing it encounters into an air-tight bottle and to label it—so is this dramatic criticism itself in turn subjected to the bottling and labelling process. A piece of criticism, however penetrating, that is not couched in the language of the commencement address of the president of Millsaps College, and that fails to include a mention of the Elizabethan theatre and a quotation from Victor Hugo's "Hernani," is labelled "journalistic." A criticism that elects to make its points with humour rather than without humour is labelled "flippant." A criticism that shows a wide knowledge of everything but the subject in hand is labelled "scholarly." One that, however empty, prefixes every name with a Mr. and somewhere in it discloses the fact that the critic is sixty-five years old is labelled "dignified." One that is full of hard common sense

[145]

from beginning to end but is guilty of wit is derogatorily labelled "an imitation of Bernard Shaw." One that says an utterly worthless play is an utterly worthless play, and then shuts up, is labelled "destructive"; while one that points out that the same play would be a much better play if Hauptmann or De Curel had written it is labelled "constructive and informing." And so it goes. With the result that dramatic criticism in America is a dead art language. Like Mr. William Jennings Bryan, it has been criticized to death.

The American mania for being on the popular side has wrapped its tentacles around the American criticism of the theatre. The American critic, either because his job depends upon it or because he appreciates that *kudos* in this country, as in no other, is a gift of the mob, sedulously plays safe. A sheep, he seeks the comfortable support of other sheep. It means freedom from alarums, a guaranteed pay envelope at the end of the week, dignity in the eyes of the community, an eventual election to the National Insti-

tute of Arts and Letters and, when he reaches
three score years and ten and his trousers have
become thin in the seat, a benefit in the Century Theatre with a bill made up of all
the eminent soft-shoe dancers and fat trage-
diennes upon whom he has lavished praise.
This, in America, is the respected critic. If
we had among us today a Shaw, or a Walkley,
or a Boissard, or a Bahr, or a Julius Bab,
he would be regarded as not quite nice.
Certainly the Drama League would not invite
him to appear before it. Certainly he would
never be invited to sit between Prof. Richard
Burton and Prof. William Lyon Phelps at the
gala banquet to Mr. D. W. Griffith. Certainly, if his writings got into the paid prints
at all, there would be a discreet editor's note
at the top to the effect that "the publication of
an article does not necessarily imply that it
represents the ideas of this publication or of
its editors."

Criticism in America must follow the bell-
cow. The bell-cow is personal cowardice, artistic cowardice, neighbourhood cowardice, or

the even cheaper cowardice of the daily and—
to a much lesser degree—periodical press.
Up to within a few years ago it was out of
the question for a dramatic critic to write
honestly of the productions of David Belasco
and still keep his job. One of the leading
New York evening newspapers peremptorily
discharged its reviewer for daring to do so;
another New York newspaper sternly in-
structed its reviewer not to make the same
mistake twice under the penalty of being cash-
iered; a leading periodical packed off its reviewer for the offence. One of the most talented critics in New York was several years
ago summarily discharged by the newspaper
that employed him because he wrote an honest
criticism of a very bad play by an obscure
playwright named Jules Eckert Goodman.
Another conscientious critic, daring mob opinion at about the same time—he wrote, as I
recall, something to the effect that the late
Charles Frohman's productions were often
very shoddy things—was charily transferred

the next day to another post on the newspaper's staff. I myself, ploughing my familiar modest critical course, have, indeed, been made not personally unaware of the native editorial horror of critical opinions which are not shared by the Night School curricula, the inmates of the Actors' Home, the Independent Order of B'nai B'rith, the United Commercial Travellers of America, and the Moose. Some years ago, a criticism of Hall Caine and of his play "Margaret Schiller," which ventured the opinion that the M. Caine was perhaps not one of the greatest of modern geniuses, so frightened the editors of the Philadelphia *North American* and the Cleveland *Leader* that I doubt they have yet recovered from the fear of the consequences of printing the review.

The ruling ethic of the American press so far as the theatre is concerned is one of unctuous *lassez faire*. "If you can't praise, don't dispraise," is the editorial injunction to the reviewer. The theatre in America is a great business—greater even than the department store—and a great business should be treated with proper respect. What if the reviewer does not admire "The Key to Heaven"? It played to more than *twelve thousand dollars* last week; it *must* be good. The theatre must be helped, and the way to help it is uninterruptedly to speak well of it. Fine drama? Art? A newspaper has no concern with fine drama and art; the public is not interested in such things. A newspaper's concern is primarily with news. But is not dramatic swindling, the selling of spurious wares at high prices, news? Is not an attempt to corrupt the future of the theatre as an honourable institution and an honourable business also news, news not so very much less interesting, perhaps, than the three column account of an ex-Follies girl's adulteries? The reviewer, for his impertinence, is assigned henceforth to cover the Jefferson Market police court.

The key-note of the American journalistic

attitude toward the theatre is a stagnant optimism. Dramatic art and the red-haired copy boy are the two stock jokes of the American newspaper office. Here and there one encounters a reviewer who, through either the forcefulness or the amiability of his personality, is successful for a short time in evading the editorial shackles—there are a few such still extant as I write. But soon or late the rattle of the chains is heard and the reviewer that was is no more. He is an American, and must suffer the penalty that an American who aspires to cultured viewpoint and defiant love of beauty must ever suffer. For—so George Santayana, late professor of philosophy in Harvard University, in "Character and Opinion in the United States"— "the luckless American who is drawn to poetic subtlety, pious retreats, or gay passions, nevertheless has the categorical excellence of work, growth, enterprise, reform, and prosperity dinned into his ears: every door is open in this direction and shut in the other; so that he either folds up his heart and withers in a corner—in remote places you sometimes find such a solitary gaunt idealist—or else he flies to Oxford or Florence or Montmartre to save his soul—or perhaps not to save it."

THE END